The Chain Imperative

The Chain Imperative

The Story of How a British Comany
Re-engineered Itself for the Future

Patrick McHugh and Paul Hannon

2000

Published in association with

Coopers
&Lybrand

First published in 1994 by Management Books 2000 Ltd
125A The Broadway, Didcot, Oxfordshire OX11 8AW

Printed and bound in Great Britain by BPC Wheatons Ltd, Exeter

British Library Cataloguing in Publication Data is available

ISBN 1-85251-197-4

Introduction

This is a management novel about how a management concept developed within a single English engineering company over a period of 70 years. It is a tale of two chains – a design chain and a manufacturing chain – which the owners of the company gradually discover run through their business regardless of major world events or the day-to-day competition around the corner.

The Dartry family, owners of Albion Engineering Ltd, discover that there are four principal dimensions of any design or manufacturing process. Starting with the interwar years, Tom Dartry learns that there are 'strategic' and 'tactical' elements required in manufacturing. It takes a later generation of the family to identify the next links in the design and manufacturing chains – the 'operational' and 'continuous' dimensions of a business. And finally there is a hint that there is a fifth dimension, a 'cultural' dimension, which perhaps precedes all the others.

The story is presented as a work of fiction, but one that is rooted firmly in the atmosphere of the times. It may be read solely as a piece of entertainment, but when read in conjunction with the chapter notes and relevant footnotes, the reader may gain a sense of the historical development of engineering theory and practice in manufacturing.

In that Albion is the ancient name for England, the story can also be seen as an allegory for the changes that British manufacturing industry has encountered during this century.

Patrick McHugh and Paul Hannon

Chapter One – 1928

Amelia Earhart flies across the Atlantic; Harrods takes over D H Evans; the Oxford English Dictionary is completed; Malcolm Campbell sets a new land speed record

A watchful Macready paced up and down the chaotic Queen Street office as a plumber worked all morning installing the machine. The nervousness of this diligent, if somewhat autocratic, Mancunian permeated the small office and it was not until the hapless plumber had successfully run the pipes and valves into the lavatory on the landing that Macready breathed an audible sigh of relief. During a lunch break he enforced on everyone else, Macready anxiously tested the pipes, found one small leak, fixed it and checked his switching until he felt nothing could fail him.

Shortly after 4 o'clock, traffic in Queen Street came to a standstill as a huge procession of private vehicles parked outside Number 22A. Office workers from adjacent buildings peered out into the street to see a constant stream of people entering the Albion Trading and Engineering Company. Volleys of raucous abuse came from some of the more persistent motorists who tried to navigate the clogged road.

As each guest arrived in the office, they were offered a glass of sherry and a lavishly printed brochure of the new appliance, and were then diplomatically guided by Tom Dartry, a long-armed stooping gangly-looking frame of a man, to the centre of the room where the laundry machine[1] stood in full view. A few inquisitive heads peered into the mechanism and appeared impressed, if slightly perplexed, by its unfamiliar appearance.

Once the room filled up, and the more serious investors had safely arrived, James Fairfax, Tom's partner and fellow officer during the Great War, took control. Fairfax, a well-lunched red-bearded sort, tapped the side of his sherry glass with an ivory letter opener.

"Gentlemen, thank you for sparing me so much of your

time." He waited for complete silence. "I assure you your attendance today will be handsomely rewarded, for you are about to see the first public demonstration of a new, and dare I say quite revolutionary, device which will transform domestic life in Great Britain.

"I crave your indulgence a little further, however, as I need a volunteer." Apart from a bit of nervous schoolboy tittering the room remained silent.

"I would like a handkerchief – nothing too out of the ordinary. Just a plain white handkerchief."

Robert D'Arby, a robust good-humoured looking man, stepped forward. "Here you are, James."

"Thank you, Robert. You'll be able to tell your grandchildren that you and your handkerchief made history today."

Everyone laughed politely.

"Now, the machine, as you may notice, is plumbed into our water supply in the hallway. But imagine a simple domestic scene. Helen, if you please."

Helen Joyce, Albion's attractive secretary and a rock of stability despite her 22 years, approached James with a silver tray. She took the handkerchief, placed it on the tray and poured a glass of sherry over it to the muffled amusement of everyone in the room. Using the sherry-soaked handkerchief, she then picked up a lump of coal from the ornate brass scuttle beside the fireplace. All eyes were now on the blackened sherry-stained linen square.

She placed the handkerchief in the washing machine tub, added some soap flakes, and signalled Tom to turn on the water. A gush of hot water poured into the machine and once the motor was running, she closed the tub's highly polished mahogany lid.

"Gentlemen," James interjected, "the only thing worse than watching paint dry must be watching your laundry being washed. May I suggest another drink while the machine looks after itself."

Helen served further sherries and retreated to the back wall. James, by now glowing with sherry and excitement, was in the middle of telling the senior partner at William Gunn & Co. a risqué story when the machine stopped. All eyes turned to look at it. A gush of water was forced out of the drain pipe.

By now standing beside the washing machine, James put his finger to his lips and turned a switch.

The washing tub, visible from the front, began to spin faster and faster until some in the room thought an accident was imminent. James had melted back into the crowd and watched the mesmerised gaze of all present. Suddenly, the motor cut out and the tub began to slow down until it finally stopped.

Helen reappeared. She lifted the mahogany lid off the machine and plucked a clean *dry* handkerchief out to the amazement of all. She handed it back to a visibly impressed D'Arby.

"I'm sorry, Robert," quipped James, "we don't have a model yet that will iron it for you."

Everyone laughed.

The carefully orchestrated demonstration had been an unqualified success. When it was followed by further, individual, presentations to key investors, the stock market launch, of both Albion Engineering and Tom Dartry's engineering chains, was underway.

Chapter Notes

The late 1920s was a period of immense optimism during which many believed the civilised world was moving towards the rule of enlightened and peace-loving democracies. Britain, with the spectre of the 1914-18 war still vivid in the national consciousness, was one of the leading proponents of international disarmament.

At the same time, the enormous prosperity of the United States offered an alluring example of domestic achievement and the overflow of American wealth provided the capital for industrial enterprise in Europe. It was the first decade in which mass production techniques began to have a serious impact on the quality of life of ordinary individuals. Now motor cars, electrically-operated domestic appliances – especially radio sets – heralded a new age of consumerism.

For Britain, however, this new age was also witness to the death throes of virtually all her old consumer goods industries; textiles, leather, pottery and woodworking were now in difficulty, while the nation's traditional economic strengths – coal mining, iron and steel, and shipbuilding – were also in trouble.

Reference Notes

[1]The increase in the number of British homes with electricity, when combined with the virtual disappearance of domestic servants after the First World War, prompted a surge in labour-saving household appliances during the 1920s. Primitive washing machines, sometimes crude gas-fired wash boilers that were agitated by hand, were replaced by models near the end of the decade with the first waterproof electric motors and with metal cabinets. However, spin driers operating on the centrifugal principle, which made their first appearance in the US during this period, were not available in Britain until the 1960s.

Many other standard household appliances date from the interwar years. Domestic refrigerators, first available in the US in the early 1920s, were sold in Britain a few years later by Frigidaire and Kelvinator. The Swedish electric appliance maker Electrolux, which set up a British subsidiary in 1921, launched a simpler and more efficient household refrigerator in Britain in 1925.

The 1920s witnessed the development of electric kettles although the electric automatic teamaker, the Hawkins Teasmade, was not marketed until 1932. Vastly improved hot water systems such as the Vivo (first sold in 1925) and the Ascot, which had its roots in the German Junkers water system (1932), made domestic life more comfortable.

In Britain, washing machines sold in small numbers in the 1920s and 1930s. Only after 1945 were they manufactured and sold in quantity. The automated washing machines with programmed cycles of washing, rinsing and spin drying became a widespread success in the 1960s. Since then models have become increasingly sophisticated, including choice of programmes to suit different fibres and biological control. (cf. *An Encyclopedia of the History of Technology*, Ian McNeil, Routledge, 1990.)

Chapter Two –Eight Months Earlier

Price of petrol hits 25-year low; Morris Motors buys Wolseley; Al Jolson stars in "The Jazz Singer"; Ford unveils the Model A; "Ain't She Sweet"

It was a dull November day, one of those occasions that makes you wonder how many shades of grey could possibly exist. Business was slow – except for some bulk orders that James had secured from Whiteleys for something that he had found in France or Belgium. Tom had drawn himself to the fireplace in the Queen Street office – several firebricks had been pulled out to enlarge the grate – but the room remained cold. Faced with the perpetual near-freezing conditions in the room and the damp coming up from the Thames, he doubted the wisdom of shaving off his beard.

Helen, his secretary, was charged with regular stoking of the fire and the necessary visits to the coal cellar. She made large mugs of tea, kept a supply of Veno's cough mixture close to hand, tried to look busy and only occasionally engaged Tom in conversation. To her mind, he was not the same man since he started his walking lark in the summer.

Curled up in front of the fire, Tom began jotting down notes with the stub of a pencil.

He was trying to give life to ideas that struck him four months before on his first walking trip to the Downs. Subsequent hikes round the Devil's Punchbowl and along the Seven Sisters saw his ideas develop but he was still uncertain how or where they would end.

On that first walk, he had let his mind wander through time, to the days at Ypres and the carnage that ensued. But there on the Downs he looked at the landscape through the eyes of a commander – although he attained only the rank of Captain in the Signal Corps – and he mused where he would have placed his battalions, where he would have dug in and how he would have supplied them. He thought about the Germans, how their supply lines had been stretched and how the Prussians had held the ridge and the village of Passchendaele until early November 1917.

His mind drifted back to the lines of communication that were so carefully constructed by the Officer Corps in general and the Signal Corps in particular. They were not unlike the rails of East Grinstead station leading back to the main station at Waterloo. Several Americans he had met during the war even suggested that the US business world was being deliberately modelled on the American railway system, with branch managers and line managers all feeding through to the trunk line and on to head office.

He remembered how the General Staff had seemed completely oblivious of the dreadful reality of the battlefield. And how he was told not to be unduly concerned about the Field Marshal's strategy; he was to worry only about tactics. Now for the first time Tom was struck with the thought that his new job at Albion also contained strategic and tactical elements, both of which needed different perspectives.

A couple of weekends later, by now better equipped with stout walking boots from Milletts, Ordnance Survey maps and bars of Bournville chocolate, Tom gazed in the distance at the railway line into Haslemere. He thought of supply lines. It was one thing to put the railway into place, to design the trains and signalling but it was something entirely different to get the goods to the station on time and to meet them from the arriving trains. As the magnificently equipped German army discovered to its cost, a battle or even a war can be lost if supplies stop reaching it.

It's not unlike my business, Tom thought. It's all very well having an office but if we don't have something people want and we don't have suppliers and customers, nothing will happen. Was there a way to link the budding Albion Engineering and Trading Company to its suppliers and customers so they all were bound together? Could he link the ideas for trade and products to potential customers? Not just one link but a series of links or chains. It seemed like he needed to pull on all things at once like a puppeteer. At times the complexity of the business almost overwhelmed him and he longed for the certitude and security of his army days.

His mind returned to strategy and tactics. Both were

necessary. Neither could exist without the other. They were linked, like parts of a chain. Yes, he mused, not a chain of command but a chain of materials and ideas. First you need a strategy, then tactics. He had to admit it wasn't the most original concept he had ever come across but he wondered how many of his contemporaries even bothered to look at business in this light.

He grudgingly admired the simplistic approach of his partner, James Fairfax, to commerce – turnover equals profit, profit equals growth and growth equals further turnover. In Tom's eyes, James was a lovable swashbuckler more at home in the eighteenth century when commerce was conducted with both ledger and sword. Here was the last of the old breed who still believed passionately in the invincibility of British industrial might. Yet Tom felt the world was changing rapidly and simplistic views of business were a dangerous thing.[1]

They had met during the final months of the war, when Tom had been knocked unconscious by a shell blast while attempting to run an emergency communications cable to their trenches. An undaunted James had drawn sniper fire away from him and later ventured back to collect his fellow officer under fire. His commendation, which cited this act of bravery, also noted the successful hooking up of the telephone link. 'Swift and Sure', the motto of the Royal Engineers Signal Service, certainly seemed to apply.

After the war, James, armed with a small inheritance from a deceased aunt, bought a derelict company with no tangible asset other than its name – Albion. He spent the next few years as a trader, buying and selling engineering components but almost went bankrupt during the 1920-21 slump when most of his customers went to the wall. He subsequently travelled around England for several years and just barely managed to keep Albion alive. A second inheritance, this time from a distant uncle who was pioneering wireless transmissions in Australia, yielded £3,000 – enough, James thought, to get Albion back on its feet.

Aware that he was running out of aunts and uncles and that Albion needed to expand, he decided to look for a partner, preferably one from his army days. Thomas Dartry was the first name that came to mind. Almost 10 years after demobilisation, he tracked Tom down in Lancashire where he was tending his father's sheep and working part-time as a clerk. He offered Tom a job and gave him an advance of 10 guineas "to buy some decent suits". James tried hard to smother a giggle when Tom appeared a few days later in the Queen Street office with his new business attire. His new partner had acquired three identical pinstripe suits, all of the same material. Placing a comradely arm around Tom's shoulder, James admitted that some army habits were hard to break.

Now sitting, shivering, in the Queen Street office, Tom slowly sipped his mug of hot tea and gathered a rug over his legs. Helen pulled a chair beside the fire and, glancing at the furrowed brow of her employer, left Tom deep in thought.

Henry Ford, Tom mused, was a man with a strategy and the right tactics to implement it. He had a goal of being the largest manufacturer of automobiles in the world and he used the principle of the production line to achieve it.[2] An automobile was a hugely complicated engineering product, yet the tactics of the production line enabled it to be simplified beyond belief.

Strategy and tactics were clearly at work here. But Tom was not satisfied with this. Again it appeared too simple a truth. There was something missing and he couldn't figure out what it was. If Tom's business strategy were to make motor cars, he would need to develop a whole arsenal of tactics to achieve that target. These could be built up over time through some trial and error and eventually he would have a profitable car manufacturing company.

The question that needed to be answered then was why there were no Henry Fords in Britain. In fact, apart from the likes of William Morris, quite the opposite seemed to be the case. The British engineering industry was littered with the remains of dozens of small car companies that had briefly flowered, then died. There was obviously more to engineering than simply making a product.

Then it struck Tom. The missing element was design!

"Of course," he said aloud. "Ford had a simple design."

"Sorry, Mr Dartry?"

"Oh, ignore me Helen. I'm just thinking aloud."

9

"You've been very quiet for a long time. Would you like some more tea?"

"Yes, that would be fine. Thank you."

Tom retreated into another deep bout of concentration. Design! Ford was using his designs as part of his strategy. A car simple enough that anyone could repair it. Who could turn down a car like that? A whole breed of owner drivers has evolved who don't need engineering degrees to keep their cars moving.

Tom started to sketch with his pencil stub. He wrote:

Design: Strategy >>>>> Tactics >>>>>

Manufacturing: Strategy >>>>> Tactics >>>>>

And the arrows of his sketch led straight into the factory. These two chains came together in Henry Ford's plant in Detroit and very probably in many other factories around the world.

When they came together they created a business.

Design obviously had a key part to play in any product. It looked certain that many great industrialists had figured this out already on the strategic level and, if some of the more humorous stories about Ford were true, he had probably figured out how to treat his design on a tactical level as well.

Tom remembered hearing a tale about the great American industrialist insisting that one of his suppliers deliver goods in packing cases of certain dimensions and that some of the sides of the case had to have holes of a specific size drilled in specific places. The obliging supplier thought nothing of it at first, but his curiosity eventually got the better of him. On a visit to the Ford plant, he followed one of his cases from the goods inward bay further down the line, where it was knocked apart, and the side with the holes drilled was suddenly hoisted up onto the production line. Ford was using the packing case, his case, as part of the Model T's flooring.

This was it, Tom thought. Strategy and tactics must operate in design and manufacturing. The genius of a company lies in combining them both. They must work in tandem. You had to look at the two chains, product design and manufacture simultaneously.

If he could put this theory into practice, he would have made a breakthrough.

"Mr Dartry, shall I fetch some more coal? Mr Dartry?"

"Oh, Helen, I'm sorry, I was miles away, thinking again."

"About Mr Ford, sir?"

"Yes, as a matter of fact, yes. He's an incredible man."

"Well, shall I get the coal?"

"Yes, but not that Coalite. Build up a good fire. I want to have a chat with you."

Helen, fair-haired and bright-eyed, looked awkwardly at her employer and his final remark. When she returned to the office with a large bucket of coal, she stoked the fire and built a thick top layer of coal followed by a thin layer of slack.

Tom had gathered his notes and stored them away safely in the indestructible Chatwood safe that James had insisted on purchasing. "Helen, apart from keeping a fire going in this office, what is the worst chore you have to do?"

She settled back into her chair, relieved that the conversation was not about more serious matters and she need not fear for her 30-shilling-a-week job.

"Do you mean here in the office, Mr Dartry, or anywhere? Because if it's anywhere, without a doubt it's washing and ironing clothes. We can't afford to have it laundered, so Florence and I are always elbow-deep in soap. And in weather like this Mr Dartry, it's difficult to dry anything."

For the next 10 minutes, Tom listened to Helen. It took him a while to figure out that his secretary was actually sharing a room in Hammersmith with someone and that conditions were far from comfortable. When she paused briefly to catch her breath Tom enquired about her regular visits to her family in Manchester.

"Oh yes, Mr Dartry, and I also pack a case every time I go see my Mam. "

The thought struck Tom as odd. Did these young women, crowding into trains at Euston, Waterloo and Liverpool Street station at weekends really carry great suitcases of dirty clothes with them. He began to ponder the absurdity of tons of laundry travelling hundreds of miles just to be washed.

"But how does your mother do it?" The question came from a man who had his own laundry sent out to a good service.

"Oh, she doesn't mind it too much. She's well used to handling baskets of washing and sometimes she gets Mr Macready to give her a hand."

"Mr Macready?"

"He's a real sweetheart, he is. I think he's a bit soft on Mam and tries to help her out a bit. He knew Dad quite well before he died."

"You mean, Mr Macready gets immersed in soap suds while he's sweet-talking your mother?"

"Heavens no, Mr Dartry. Mr Macready is the maintenance supervisor at the Stanley Laundry in Manchester. He's a brilliant mind when it comes to those big machines. He's working on the machines all the time, but he saves the big jobs for weekends and bank holidays and sometimes throws in a batch of our clothes to test the washers."

"He can take those machines apart blindfolded," Helen ventured, "and put them back before you know it. Mr Macready says these new American machines are the thing of the future, except they keep breaking down. He's even promised to build a machine that will wash and dry clothes as a birthday present for Mam."

Tom found himself staring at Helen again. He slipped into thought as she stoked up the fire and placed another thin layer of coal dust on the hot coals. "Well, I think your Mr Macready sounds like a genius. I'd like to meet him. He might be able to help me with a little problem I've been thinking about."

The following morning, Queen Street had its usual bustle of pedestrian and road traffic. It was almost 9.30 and the bobbing up and down of figures, many in straw boaters and some in bowlers, produced a shimmering effect on the eye. An occasional private car darted between the Number 9 buses and the slow-moving horse-drawn delivery vans. Only the brave and the alert cared to cross through the shunting erratic train of vehicles.

Tom found the office already open. Sitting with his feet up on their partners' desk was James, his hands resting lightly on his stomach. The smoke from a small cigar curled toward the ceiling. With both eyes still closed, he signalled to Tom to come nearer. From the untidy state of James's well-tailored suit, Tom wondered whether he might have slept in it.

Chapter Two

A signwriter, painstakingly outlining the huge italic A of Albion on the window, dangled his feet inside the room. Noise from Queen Street – in various forms but principally the chugging of cars up the hill from Southwark Bridge and the clatter of hooves along the thoroughfare – rushed into the office and made conversation difficult.

Tom, shuffling from side to side, kept his overcoat on in a vain attempt to fend off the cold air pouring in through the open window.

"What's wrong, Tom?" James asked. "You look gloomier than usual."

Whenever Tom felt cold or particularly self-conscious he hunched up his tall frame and dangled his yard-long arms at his sides like a depressed spider. "Don't get me wrong, James," he began.

James's eyes, piercing through cigar smoke, bore in on his partner and fellow officer.

"I thought it would be different, that's all," Tom ventured with a note of hesitation in his voice.

"What's really the matter, Tom?"

"I'm not cut out for the type of trading you do. I don't know how to buy and sell flanges or cogs or machines, but I think I know how to make them. James, we're supposed to be an engineering company but we don't make anything."

"Is that it? Is that all that's bothering you?"

"Yes."

"Well, of course Albion is a trading company at the moment. That's where all the profit comes from. I want to expand and need you to look at new ideas. If you want to manufacture something, let's find something to make."

"I've found it!"

"My word, we have been busy. Well, tell me?"

"Washing machines!"

"Have you come unhinged, dear boy?"

"Washing machines like they've never been made before. In a modern, scientific and highly profitable way."

"Thank God! For a minute, I thought you'd lost your marbles."

"But first, I must tell you about my theory of chains!"

Reference Notes

[1]Among the early pioneers of the systematic analysis of management and industrial problems was John McAdam (1756-1836), best known as a road maker. He travelled the country at his own expense and investigated existing road-making practices. He found some roads were poor because they were constructed with a mixture of stones of all sizes and shapes, held together with mud. They were badly shaped, high in the middle, steeply cantered at the sides and seldom properly drained. He also found that wagon wheels tended to rock the large stones, especially if they were rounded, that mud acted as a lubricant and that weak spots developed into dangerous ruts.

He decided that a road should be made of stones of uniform size and that they should be broken into pebbles and laid as a carpet on properly shaped and drained foundation. These principles of road making hold good today, the only difference being that tar is used to bind the stones together hence the term 'tar macadam'.

McAdam insisted that good road making could only be done by properly paid and trained workmen, under the direction of a skilled and properly paid supervisor. In his view, it was no economy, indeed worse than useless, to employ unpaid (convict) and casual labour.

McAdam's breakthrough in systematic analysis quite literally paved the way for much of the later thought on management theory.

Ranked among the greatest nineteenth century thinkers on management theory was Charles Babbage (1791-1871). Babbage was the first to suggest that the principles of scientific method ought to be applied to all management problems. In his opinion, the skill and knowledge required for successful industrial enterprise were not intuitive or empirical, but had to be scientific in character and based on exact knowledge, systematically collected and analysed, and he endeavoured to define the principles upon which the industrialist, applying sound economic theory and the latest technical improvements, should organise production so as to secure maximum efficiency.

Much of Babbage's contribution to management theory is contained in *The Economy of Machinery and Manufacture,* published in 1832. In spite of the popularity of his book, editions of which were published in Europe and in the US, he is chiefly remembered for his 'difference engine', the fore-runner of the modern computer.

[2]By the 1920s, the development of the modern consumer society was well under way and the emergence of the owner-driver was beginning to be recognised as an important trend in motoring.

The Financial Times' motoring correspondent noted in January 1921:

"Before the war, the man who kept a chauffeur, even if the latter drove but seldom, cared little for chassis accessibility, for instance. It did not concern him that the fan-belt drive was not provided with any easy means of adjustment, or that the undershield, once let down, would take a man a good hour to attach and cause a week's annoyance to be crowded into that hour.

"To-day, this is all changed, for the majority of owners now like to look after their cars themselves, and appreciate such an asset as accessibility, because it means that their adjustment or repair bill is less in proportion."

At the lower end of the new car market a four-seater Morris Oxford sold for £595 whereas an Austin Twenty was priced at £850, an imported Buick was available at £745 and a particularly swift Vauxhall (top speed 70 mph) was priced at £1,300.

In the US, the carmakers of Detroit were busy jockeying for position and in the process were shaping the industrial landscape of twentieth-century America. Henry Ford, who had set up his first moving production line in 1913, had by the middle of the 1920s seen his early lead in the motor industry whittled away by competitors like General Motors. GM was intent on building up a full range of automobiles to match the different purchasing power of various segments of the public. This contrasted sharply with Ford's own spartan approach to the introduction of new models. Somewhat belatedly, Ford decided to close down production for almost an entire year in order to set up a new plant for the Model A. Some industry observers have suggested that the Ford company never fully recovered from this shutdown. In this case, Ford's decision, doubtless based on sound tactical commercial reasons, proved to have profound long-term strategic implications.

Chapter Three – 1928

Britain renounces war; Tipperary Tim wins the Grand National; Elastoplast sticking plasters; "Ol' Man River"

In the early months of 1928, James Fairfax moved his arcane, but immensely profitable, trading activities into top gear. Operating mainly from the plush, reassuring rooms of the Delphinium Gentlemen's Club in Pall Mall, he bought, sold and bartered on a huge scale to accumulate capital for Albion's new engineering venture.

Ball bearings were traded for pulleys, which in turn were bartered for Sugden Superheaters and then converted into chemicals and sold for cash. A small Brazilian hardwood forest was purchased from a member of the Delphinium and then swapped for a second-hand steam ship in Uruguay. Once the rusting vessel had successfully completed the hazardous trans-atlantic journey and off-loaded its valuable cargo of ripe bananas in Le Havre, James exchanged it for a French steam locomotive, which he duly sold a week later for cash.

With James, iron ore could become surgical instruments just as easily as out-of-season bananas could become accommodation at the Savoy. Coal was swapped for straw which was exchanged for paper and then for corrugated cardboard. Within a few weeks, James controlled a large slice of the infant London corrugated packaging market.

Although the Delphinium frowned on business being conducted on its premises, most members turned a blind eye to James's constant meetings with often seedy looking characters. In their eyes he was a larger-than-life character and allowances needed to be made for him.[1] Furthermore, he occasionally had interesting business propositions and there was, of course, the nightly copy of the *Financial News* to look forward to.

An obscure rule of the club forbade evening newspapers – although it was a moot point whether the first edition of the next day's paper was covered by this regulation – so the nightly *FN* was navigated with impeccable agility by a member of staff from table to table. Silently the newspaper was scrutinised and then left to be ferried on to the next expectant reader. Only once was its presence alluded to when one evening a muffled and exasperated "Godddd!" was muttered. By the end of the evening, most had read that one of their number was teetering on the edge of bankruptcy.

Tom acted as the newspaper courier. He endeavoured to meet James each evening, usually after working late in Queen Street or after seeing Helen home to Hammersmith. He would make a detour to the *FN* offices in Bishopsgate where he would pick up a copy of the first edition of the following morning's newspaper. Then, having hailed a taxi, he would hurtle around the small back streets of the City as if rehearsing a scene from a Keystone Kops film.

Late one evening in March 1928, Tom and James met in the Delphinium to assess their progress. James was fingering a poorly rolled cigar and bemoaning, in Tom's estimate for the millionth time, the passing of Van Raalte's tobacconist in Piccadilly.

As two men headed into the smoking room, the *FN* had already been picked up by the head porter and was beginning to make its discreet evening rounds of the club.

"I don't think I can raise the £30,000 we need, Tom. I'm sorry."

"What's the problem?"

"I'm stuck with tons of Egyptian cotton.[2] All my cash is tied up in it. If I could unload that, we'd be sailing. I just can't complete the circle. But there may be another way." James's eyes scanned the smoking room.

"You mean some of the club members?" Tom probed.

"Well, yes and no. I was thinking of the stock market. Sell three-quarters of Albion through a public share issue. Our accounts and trading record are healthy enough to meet any Stock Exchange rules."

"But the market, James, it's a thieves kitchen."

"Tom, there's enough old money in this room that isn't adverse to making new money, so long as their sensibilities are not disturbed," James announced in a well-informed tone. "The stock market is the most respectable way to get them involved in the company and raise the money we need."

"How much control would we have?"

"We'll remain major shareholders and effectively run the company on a day-to-day basis. There's no shame in going to the market, it's a sign of coming of age. Some of the greatest names in the history of business are listed on the London Stock Exchange."[3]

"Is there any alternative?"

"Not if you want to see your chain theory in practice by the end of the year. Now tell me about Macready. Did he finally agree terms?"

"Well, like you said, no royalties or anything like that. Straight deal, lump sum."

"How much?"

"Less than we feared. I stressed that proper trials would have to take place and we'd pay for the necessary development work. His eyes lit up when I told him we wanted other ideas that would form part of the Macready Range. I made it sound as if we were creating another Mr Hoover or Mr Diesel."

"You did well, but how much?"

"His asking price. Two hundred pounds. Over a year's pay for him. And I promised a retainer of 50 shillings a week after the first year to work on new projects – in his own time, in his own shed."

"My God, what kind of monster have I created?" James's nose almost twitched with delight at Tom's success.

"I'm off to Manchester tomorrow to meet Helen's mother. I've got lodgings near Macready so we can work on the machine together."

"You seem to be making rather swift progress with Helen, old boy." James noted. "A very pretty girl, it'll be a pity to lose her."

The following afternoon, Tom met Samuel Macready again in his leaky garden shed which was dominated by an old cast-iron stove, on which sat a copper kettle and a soldering iron. A well-used ink-stained drawing board, which Macready explained had been picked up cheaply at auction and which now acted as a table, occupied one corner of the shed. While Macready brewed tea, Tom fiddled with the board, which in his view looked like it had deserved a well-earned retirement from the drawing office.[4]

Under the window stood a five-foot wooden workbench with an eight-inch engineer's vice and a wooden vice. The top of the bench was strewn with saws, hammers, taps, dies, wrenches and old Oxo boxes.

There were four ageing doorless cupboards which Tom half-suspected had also been picked up at auction. They bulged with a huge assortment of spare parts and leftovers. One had what Macready termed fix-ups – screws and fasteners – while another had odd plumbing bits. A third was stuffed full of electrical connections and the last held drill bits and jig saws.

There were also two old red armchairs, tired and sagging and slightly blackened with oil from grubby overalls. The wall opposite the door was covered entirely with a jumble of half completed inventions, cannibalised parts, 'homers'[5] and twisted coils of wire.

Tom sat rather gingerly as he was handed a mug of tea. He looked up at the bars of steel and planks of wood suspended above his head. Chaos reigned supreme. After staring at some of the equipment and partially-finished prototypes for a while, one could detect which had been designed by Samuel Macready. Macready's creations bore the hallmark of simplicity.

Tom spotted a meat grinder, a cream separator and an unusual combination of gears, which Macready described as an "automatic gear change" for a motor car. Tom scratched his head in wonder.

Both men clutched their mugs. Macready, in his early fifties and looking every bit the inveterate boffin and amateur inventor, brushed the hand tools aside and sat on the work bench with his legs dangling over the side. Tom now began to explain his theories on design and manufacturing.

"You see, Mr Macready, what we design should be influenced by how we can best make it, rather than simply designing it for its own sake. Take a fan for example. If you wanted to cool something you'd estimate the heat you needed to carry away, but then what? Would you ask the works if they already had a fan that would do the job? Or would you go to a catalogue to see if you could buy one off the shelf with the right air flow?"

"But there's another way," Tom announced. "Would you change the design, maybe by cutting away some nearby parts, and let convection cool the area? Design it so it didn't need a fan. This way costs less and is easier for everyone."

Macready remained impassive.

"This is the chain that I was taking about," Tom tried again. "Every thing we do now will affect the profitability of the company for years to come. We've always got to bear this in mind. A simple thing like putting screws in the wrong place might cost us a fortune later. Even the choice of screws, brass or steel, could be important later." He wasn't convinced his message was getting through. He hoped for the best and realised that Macready had his own way of doing things. "Mr Macready, do you understand what I'm trying to do? We must design a machine that is easy to make, to sell, to service and, if necessary, to scrap."

Macready visibly shuddered at the word 'scrap'.

"And do you understand what I'm trying to do, Mr Dartry?" Macready huffily replied. "I've spent years trying to get this idea right, now you want to add on all of these other things."

"It's not adding on anything," Tom pleaded with him, "It's simply being aware of things further down the production line. If we make small changes at this stage, we'll save money when we manufacture it."

Macready grimaced a little, hopped down from the work bench and said they had better get to work.

His laundry machine design – like almost everything he made – was inherently simple if a little unorthodox. The tub of the machine, instead of being made of wood or galvanised metal, would be built of layers of copper, which would retain most of the heat from the washing water. This tub would be fitted with an auxiliary motor, which would run at different speeds and spin the water out first, then spin dry the clothes.[6]

Although Macready's idea was simple, his technique of working was not. Tom saw that his new designer thrived on chaos. He knew he would need to improvise his chain theory as the design took shape, but now began to see the problem of looking at every single action from four, maybe five, different perspectives. As the design took shape, the chaos and uncertainty grew exponentially. For Tom, it was a nightmare.

He and Macready worked on outline drawings to determine what the washer would look like. Draftsmanship was not a strong point for either man. At Macready's suggestion the rough plans were given to a junior draftsman at Daniel Adamson's, the boilermaker in Duckingfield. The finished detailed drawings were more pleasing to the eye than any of the cigarette packet sketches Tom or Macready had used, yet neither of the men could be certain that all the pieces were there.

"Copper rivets is the answer," Macready said later as he sketched a rough cross-section of an onion shape on the back of a packet of Woodbines to show how the skins of copper, which would absorb the heat, were to be held together.

Tom looked doubtful. "Yes, Mr Macready, but they'll be difficult to repair if something goes wrong."

"Prototypes are always difficult. Like pulling teeth, Mr Dartry, you've got to have the stomach for it." Tom wondered what dental analogies had to do with making laundry machines, but he consented to Macready hiring a coppersmith who had just been laid off from a local Manchester brewery.

Fine precision coppersmithing would be necessary as the gap between each layer of the cylinder was designed to be no more than one-sixteenth of an inch. The first layer was made without difficulty but the second and third layers ran into problems immediately. Copper from another supplier appeared to differ from the first batch ordered. Tests on the copper sheets suggested that it was tainted with impurities that would affect conductivity. New copper was requested. Further delays took place. Tom made a note of the type of quality control he would need to have over raw materials.

In the event, the coppersmith, more accustomed to maintaining the enormous vats in the Western Ale brewing hall, proved incapable of working to such fine tolerances. Tom began looking for a replacement while Macready lurched from one setback to another. Some of the parts specified could not be obtained so Macready borrowed a couple of valves from the Stanley Laundry stores. The valves, however, were so large that a hasty redesign was needed to accommodate them.

What could go wrong seemed to go wrong. When Macready ordered a jig, in this case a half-inch-thick circular piece of solid steel with a number of holes drilled into it, only four of the six holes lined up. He sent it back to be reworked. Another delay.

The copper tubing he ordered was delivered as five-eighths of an inch rather than the three-quarter inch specified. The 12 dozen six-inch bolts made a brief guest appearance in his shed as six dozen 12-inch bolts. Brass castors were found to be unsuitable, so the hunt was on for strong, rubber covered wheels.

Slowly, the pieces came together – literally. It was beyond Tom's experience to see apparently useless piles of parts and equipment build up. He assumed that design engineering was a more precise skill. But now, tripping over mounds of scrap copper in the shed, he almost panicked.

Miraculously one morning, Macready announced it was finished. Tom, looking at the pile of wires dangling from the back of the machine, was a bit hesitant. "Are you quite sure?"

"Watch." Macready plugged in the machine and poured in a kettle of hot water. He dropped in a dirty tea towel, some soap shavings he had prepared from a bar of Pear's and switched on the motor. Tom stared at the much maligned copper cylinder as it began to agitate and then gather speed. "Now," said Macready, "imagine the washing is finished." He flipped a switch that turned off the agitating cylinder and allowed it to slow down.

He unplugged the bottom of the cylinder to allow the water to pour out. "When this is connected to a drain, it will look much better," Macready said anxiously. "Here is where it really happens." With the plug hole still open, the cylinder began to rotate again, this time steadily building up speed until it looked like a reddish-orange blur. Both men were doused by a fine spray of water coming from its open top.

"It needs a top," Tom shouted above the whirring sound. "And it's a bit loud." Macready just nodded.

After five minutes, Macready turned off the motor and the cylinder began to slow down and finally lurched to a halt. He delicately dipped his hand into the cylinder, extracted the freshly washed, and by now almost completely dry, tea towel, and handed it to Tom, who fingered it and looked Macready in the face. "You've done it, haven't you?"

"I think so," said Macready, almost pink with pride and excitement. "We'll need to run a few more tests though."

"Yes, and you might have a look at the size of it," Tom suggested. "It's bigger and louder than I thought." Macready's face pinched slightly at what he considered to be a significant design change. He scratched his head, slowly mouthing the words 'big and loud'.

"Mr Macready, ordinary people like you and me are going to buy these machines for our homes. They're not going into factories. They've got to be smaller and quieter."

"Smaller and quieter," Macready said quietly. "We'll see what we can do, Mr Dartry."

Tom put on his overcoat and hat and went to telephone James in London. By now beginning to feel a bit queasy with excitement, he shouted into the mouthpiece: "I think we've done it." The excitement was infectious and James wanted to know when he could see the machine in London. A demonstration would need to be arranged for members of the Delphinium Club as soon as possible.

While James courted his Pall Mall investors, Tom went looking for an empty factory and Macready, instilled also with a sense of excitement and urgency, set about refining his creation.

In trying to make the laundry machine quieter, he stuffed the metal cabinet surrounding the motor with cotton wool but it made no appreciable difference to the roaring sound of the motor. He expanded the size of the cabinet to pack in more cotton, but calculated that the dimensions of the machine would increase in proportion to the reduction in the sound levels.

He pulled the engine cowling from his new car to see how Mr Austin's engineering team had solved their problem. He tried rubber washers and seals to absorb the vibrations on the washing machine but this had only a minor impact. He tried lining the cabinet with lead and putting in a counter rotating shaft but these solutions were vetoed by Tom on grounds of cost.

Eventually Macready discovered the answer lay in the electric motor itself. He found that the copper tub was an effective sound insulator so he placed the motor under the rotating cylinder and lagged the space around the motor. This solution, however, required him to have an unusually flat motor with sturdy bearings to take the weight of the tub and a full wash-load.

Undaunted, he set about making his own electric motor and included the necessary capacitor into the motor housing. "It'll avoid any short circuits if the cylinder leaks," he joked with Tom.[7]

By early June, Macready and Tom were ready with the prototype Two-In-One Laundrymatic – a name conjured up at the last moment – and James was invited to see the new machine in its birthplace.

The shed was tidied up as much as possible – a large pile of scrap was swiftly dumped out of the window into the garden – and a flowery print curtain was hastily draped over the invention.

Standing in the doorway of the shed with a bag of laundry slung over his shoulder, James appeared somewhat bemused by the intensely rural feeling to the event. He caught sight of a bottle of sherry and glasses on a tray near the stove.

Introductions were made and finally the moment of truth arrived. Tom and Macready, with a flourish of amateur stage theatrics, pulled off the curtain to reveal the new machine.

"Hmmmh, interesting. Show me," said James offering the bag of clothes to Macready.

"Can't do all that, sir. About half that amount will work," Macready replied in a matter of fact manner.

Tom felt his stomach tighten as he looked at the tiny handful of washing Macready pushed into the machine. He remembered the armies of women carrying washing home to their mothers. Macready's device would take an entire day to wash a suitcase of clothes.

Macready nervously cleared his throat. He poured in five gallons of water and shut the lid. With another flourish, which this time made him look like an amateur magician, he pushed a large button on the side. The machine sprang to life.

During the 20-minute wash cycle, the three men chatted amiably and Macready dusted off some of his engineering concoctions to show James. And in due course, Macready triggered the drying phase of the cycle with the flipping of several switches. At the end of it, he dipped in his fingers and picked out three handkerchiefs and two shirts. He handed them to James, who nodded and passed them to Tom.

"Well?" Macready asked.

Neither James nor Tom answered. Sensing something was wrong, Macready pursued them with his eyes. "Mrs Duckett!" he exploded. "If there's something amiss, you'd better tell me. Damn it, what is it?" he shouted.

"It's too small. We've made the blasted thing too small," Tom retorted.

Macready gritted his teeth. "You told me to make it smaller and quieter. I've done that. You never said how much washing it should do."

"Sam, it's not your fault. It's mine. I thought it would carry a bigger load. At least we know now and not later. It shows the whole point of what I've being talking about. One small mistake and it's good night Lillie Langtry."

James, who had remained silent during this exchange, now spoke: "All is not lost, Mr Macready. But let me be perfectly clear, does this machine work properly?"

"Oh, yes, Mr Fairfax, without a doubt."

"Well, Mr Macready," James continued, "do whatever is necessary to get it ready for production. I think we've just seen one of Tom Dartry's chains in operation. Poor design wreaks havoc with production and sales. A good lesson!"

"Tomorrow," James commanded, "you start working on the Mark II. Cheer up Sam, it's a wonderful machine. There's nothing like it."

Macready could not be coaxed out of his depression, so Tom went for a short walk with James in Macready's garden.

"What do you think, Tom?"

"He said the size of the tub was dictated by the weight of the clothes needed to be dried and by the capacity of the motors, which keep burning out. He's already started to build his own motors," Tom offered.

Stroking his beard, James mused for a while. "We'll have to sell it differently. If it can only do a small load, we'll aim it at young couples who are too busy to hand wash but maybe are not happy sending out everything to the laundry. You know how sensitive the British nation is about its underclothes. It's

25

big enough to do socks, underwear and shirts. Once Macready produces the Mark II, we introduce our family-size version. But, for the moment, we have to catch the market with what we've got."

"Why can't we wait for the Mark II?" Tom asked anxiously.

"Impossible!" James countered. "The competition is already gathering. I mentioned the idea to Harpers in Sloane Street. They said sniffily they had heard some Americans were working on such an idea, and asked was ours from the States? One hundred per cent English, I said, and backed by a local company, not one that's thousands of miles away. We'll show them how good British engineering can be!"

Within a fortnight, as promised, James had generated a wave of interest in the new washing machine from important parts of the City and from many of his fellow club members. He extended an invitation to each of them for a grand trial demonstration of the device, which in his hyperbole was described as 'the most important household technical achievement since the vacuum cleaner'.

Reference Notes

[1]James Fairfax was carrying on a long tradition of rascal/entrepreneur that had effectively oiled the wheels of the British economy for almost two centuries. The national attitude towards men like Fairfax had been distilled by Adam Smith (1723-1790), often called the father of modern economics. Although Smith did not favourably view the motives of merchants and businessmen (he wrote,"People of the same trade seldom meet together, even for merriment and diversion, but the conversation ends in a conspiracy against the public, or in some contrivance, to raise prices.") his major thesis in *The Wealth of Nations* was that, except for limited functions, the state should refrain from interfering with the economic life of a nation. Smith argued that economic growth, which depends on capital accumulation and an increased division of labour, would be best promoted by private rather than public efforts.

[2]By the end of the 1920s, there was a huge rise in demand for man-made fibres and many natural materials such as cotton and wool temporarily lost their share of the market.

[3]In fact, the early months of 1928 saw a explosion of activity in the North American stock market which filtered back to London and other European bourses.

Although the popular image of the London Stock Exchange was that of a clubby group of gamblers who benefited at the expense of the general public – as recently as 1920, the playing of roulette within the Exchange had been forbidden by its administrators – there was immense public speculation for the rush of new industrial share issues. During 1928 as a whole, 1,172 new share issues raised £1.057 billion on the London stock market but about one half of these were not offered to the public. Those issues that sought public subscription were warmly received.

The period was also one of intense industrial agglomeration which had seen, in a matter of a few years, the creation of Imperial Chemical Industries, Cable and Wireless, and Unilever.

[4]In the 1920s, a career in a drawing office was considered highly desirable and respectable. The head of a drawing office was the Chief Draftsman who had section leaders and draftsmen under him. These men were time-served and did most of the original drawings and calculations such as machinery tolerances.

Lower down the hierarchy were tracers whose main job was to copy existing drawings that needed modification or repair as they became worn. Tracers also put in the details such as cross-hatchings or sectioning marks and prepared parts lists.

[5]On the engineering shop floor, craftsmen considered 'homers' as a natural right or perk of their jobs. Although actually illegal, it was custom and practice for men to make or repair items for home on the company's equipment and often during working hours.

[6]During the nineteenth century, many and varied attempts were made to design a washing machine. The first patent for a machine to 'wash, press out water and to press linen and wearing apparel' was taken out as early as 1780 by a Mr Rogerson from Warrington, Lancashire, but it is not clear whether the machine was ever made. Other ideas followed but it was not until after 1850 that serious attempts were made to manufacture a working machine.

Between 1850 and the early years of the twentieth century a number of different washing machines were manufactured but they were all hand-powered and manually operated. The filling and emptying had to be done by hand and, in most models, the water had to be heated first. Soap was chopped up manually and added to the hot water.

The design of the late nineteenth-century machines varied considerably, but they were all based on the traditional method of washing, using a dolly stick and washboard. The mechanisms which were devised to achieve the agitation of the water ranged from a machine which could be rocked by the foot like a cradle to one which incorporated a dolly stick attached to the lid or base of the tub; in others, the washing was churned round by paddles or pegged wooden rollers. Apart from the rocking model, the motive power was provided by a lever operated by hand. Many designs had corrugated interior walls or floors to simulate the washboard action. Most were made of wood and shaped like a tub or box. Metal was used for stands and fittings.

By the 1880s, a few machines were being made which could heat the water in the tub either by gas jets or a coal-fired boiler. The first electrically powered machines were made in the US soon after 1900. In early models the existing machine was adapted with the addition of an electric motor and this was often sited beneath the tub – a dangerous procedure as many tubs leaked and the machines were rarely earthed.

It was the late 1920s before the American washing machine was redesigned to take full advantage of electrical power and to meet the needs of the mass market. An all-metal tub replaced wooden versions and this was enclosed in an enamelled cabinet. There were two chief methods of making the washing active. One agitated the water by a revolving disc fitted with fins mounted in the hollow of the tub and operated by a driving mechanism beneath. The other was a perforated cylinder which was driven to rotate first one direction then the other. (cf. *An Encyclopedia of the History of Technology*, Ian McNeil, Routledge, 1990.)

[7]The breakthrough in washing machine design was achieved on the strength of earlier technical achievements in motor technology. Among the critical successes in this field was the development of the first practical AC, or alternating current, motor by Nikola Tesla (1856-1943) in 1888. Born in Croatia, he emigrated in 1884 to the US where he worked for a time with Edison, the leading exponent of

DC, or direct current, systems in the country and then joined Westinghouse, the leading name in AC systems.

Tesla showed that an induction or synchronous motor could be run from a single-phase supply if part of the field winding was connected through a capacitor or inductor to give a second phase. Once started, such a motor will run satisfactorily on a single-phase supply. Westinghouse bought Tesla's patents and by 1892 was manufacturing AC motors and promoting AC power systems.

In the twentieth century, most electrical motor power comes from induction motors. In an induction motor, the rotating member is not a permanent magnet and turns at a speed slightly slower than the speed of the rotating field created by the stationary coils. Currents are then induced in the motor and these interact with the rotating field to provide the driving force.

For the moment, however, the commercial success of Albion would lie in its introduction of a unique technical and commercial design at a time when the British consumer goods market was relatively unsophisticated but none the less potentially highly profitable.

Chapter Four – 1929

St Valentine's Day Massacre; Wyatt Earp dies, aged 80;
British Bentleys win at Le Mans; Black Thursday; "Tip-Toe
Through The Tulips"

The Stock Market reaction to Albion was extraordinary. Admittedly it was early 1929 and the world's markets, particularly New York and London, were steaming ahead in one of the greatest bull markets in history. For those looking for a quick kill, Albion's four shilling flotation share price rose steadily to finish the day at a one shilling premium. By any standard, the flotation was a success.

The fact that Albion was not actually manufacturing a product at this stage failed to worry any large body of investors. It was a sign of the speculative times when companies with a good business idea, and the right connections, could find sufficient finance to put the idea into practice. It had already happened with Charles Hatry's photo-booth concept, greyhound racing and even telephone services in the far-away Orient.

Both of Albion's partners had profited handsomely from the flotation. James, always hankering after the life of landed gentry, purchased a Tudor-style house in Piltdown, Sussex, while Tom, who had by now made a proposal of marriage to his secretary Helen, rented a large flat in Wimbledon and bought a sturdy second-hand six-cylinder Napier for £2,000.

Once the flotation was safely behind them, the two partners busied themselves with establishing the new Albion. As Tom hunted for a factory, James kept up his commodity trading acrobatics in order to give Albion some income and to pay the wages of its recently recruited sales representative.

Albion's competition did not take them seriously at first. Baker Perkins, the Peterborough-based specialist engineering company, had a small laundry machine subsidiary, but its market, at least for now, did not appear threatened by Albion. Friendly rivalry and a mutual respect developed between them. The fact that one of the Baker directors also controlled a small, publicly-quoted, car company called Albion Motors seemed to bring the two rivals a little bit closer.

Rivalry of a more intense nature developed with Empire Engineering, a well-established north London company. Empire prided itself on the range of household products it made and the distribution network it had built up to service over 20 countries, in effect the British Empire. Founded in 1851, the year of the Great Exhibition, Empire thrived as Britain's world trade mushroomed. But the 1914-18 war proved to be a watershed for the company as most of its senior management heeded the call to arms, duly took up firing positions in Flanders and became casualties within the first year. The company had been left in the hands of young, and somewhat inexperienced, managers to whom the relatives of the deceased board now turned to see if their investment, and future financial security, were safe. The most promising among this group of managers, who were in effect no more than young articled clerks, were 23-year-old Richard Woods and his younger half-brother Arthur. Both suffered from the same family trait of perspiring too much and always appearing to be in need of a shave. In early 1916, these two were the only commercial hope for Empire if it were to remain an independent company.

The two Woods did not disappoint their ever watchful owners. Realising that military work was the most secure source of income, Richard and Arthur first produced an effective gas mask for civilians as fears of gas attacks swept London and the south-east. Their second stroke of luck occurred in June 1917 when London was bombed for the first time by German aircraft. The speed of the aeroplanes, which gave them a greater element of surprise compared with the slower moving and more vulnerable Zeppelins, now meant that the capital needed an early warning system. Empire was the first to mass-produce air raid sirens and in turn the Woods duly achieved control of the company.

The post-war boom of 1919-20 consolidated the commercial fortunes of Empire sufficiently for it to weather the subsequent recession and during the rest of the decade Empire expanded its manufacturing and trading activities throughout the

English-speaking world. However, as their commercial prowess increased, the two Woods became increasingly intolerant of competition. A reputation for astute business practices gradually degenerated into one of sabotage, intolerance and, at times, stepping in grey areas of the law in order to discredit competitors. Only the brave, or the foolhardy, would engage the Woods lightly.

Now Empire seethed as it watched Albion change from a trader to a manufacturer and duly gave Albion's hard-pressed rep a rough passage.

Initially unaware of the uncompromising nature of Empire's business techniques, Tom and James busied themselves with a lively argument over the location of Albion's new factory. Mindful of the strategic importance of factory location in his chain theory, Tom saw the need to locate in the Midlands – one of the traditional engineering centres of Britain. James was equally insistent that they should be near to the crucial London market and close to his club. Little compromise was possible, so both got their own way.

Albion would in effect be split into two functional centres, with the Midlands concentrating on research, design engineering, manufacturing and assembly plus a small amount of warehousing. The London centre would have substantially more warehousing and sufficient space would be given over, or leased, to James's import and export business enterprise, Albion Trading, which had been hived off from the old Albion Trading and Engineering Company.

In the Midlands, spare industrial space was found in Mansfield which Tom agreed to lease, in contrast to the London premises – a rambling series of small interlinking warehouses on the Old Kent Road in south-east London – which James decided to purchase outright.

The Mansfield factory, located just outside the town, had been hurriedly built, like so many factories dotted around the industrial girdle of Britain, to make munitions during the critical 'shell shortage' late in the 1914-18 war. After the war, it had been converted to a small car assembly plant by two enterprising local men named Wheeler who knew more about the mechanics of motorcars than the business of selling them.[1] They had been entrepreneurial enough to register a patent for one of their innovations but this proved to be their high point in the motor trade. By 1921, in the middle of the post-war slump, they shut up shop and only managed to pay off bank loans by the sale of their patent to Lucas, the lighting and car accessory company.

The factory, about 40,000 square feet of space, had been modified in parts by the previous owners but large areas of it were still sectioned off by thick dividing walls, built originally to cushion the impact of explosions. More brick walls – built in the Flemish bond manner for extra strength – would need to be demolished to create a usable working area.

Tom was now faced with his first tactical decision of the production chain. At one end of the main assembly area was a two-storied brick structure used for offices. He decided that part of the electrical assembly work could be conducted on the top floor and that the ground floor offices would be retained for administration.

With Tom busy setting up the factory, James accelerated the promotion of the Two-in-One Laundrymatic. He concentrated on large retailers with whom he had developed some business associations – the Gamages, Selfridges, Harrods and Whiteleys of this world. But everywhere he found signs that Empire had been one step ahead of him, poisoning the water-hole.

When he heard that Empire was undercutting any price that Albion Trading made on any product, James counter-attacked. He promised Empire's customers that he would not only match any price Empire made, but would offer better quality as well. Over a glass of whisky one evening, he muttered to Tom: "These buggers have to be taught a lesson!"

Quietly, James liquidated his holdings of cotton, sugar, cardboard, cars, engines, timber, and God knows what else. These he converted into best-quality American, Swedish and German household goods that he could barter but while he was waiting delivery of these goods Empire lowered their prices even further. He matched them.

Certain that Empire was now losing money, James played his trump card. He flooded the market with high quality goods at the cheapest possible price. Empire was powerless to respond.

"Ha!" he scowled. "They can cut prices, but let's see if they can raise their quality."

Empire, aware it was losing scores of customers every day, reluctantly signalled a truce. For the very brief period that the truce held, James worked frantically to build a customer base that Albion's manufacturing side could eventually tap.

As part of the lease on the Mansfield factory, Albion also had the use of a cottage opposite the main factory gate. Viewing this as ideal temporary accommodation, Tom moved in with Helen, his suitcase, tennis racket and small box of books. Armed with liberal quantities of Windolene, and a host of other cleaning agents, Helen set to scouring out the cottage. A recent Harrods' sale had provided a few pieces of respectable looking furniture and the kitchen was soon crowded with a Macready washing machine and a host of his more obscure domestic appliances. Within a few weeks of settling into the cottage, Helen and Tom were married. James, in a characteristic display of generosity, gave the young couple a Philips radiogram as a wedding present.

Living adjacent to the plant, Tom visited it often and mused how impressive it would look once the safety brick walls had been demolished and how the factory floor, dotted with iron piers, would be flooded with sunlight from the skylights.

Tom now moved onto the next crucial ingredient in his production chain. Located two miles down the road were the industrial premises of Arthur C. Ball & Co., which made components for the Austin motor car company. One evening, at the end of the day shift, he visited the pub adjacent to the factory. He struck up an easy conversation with some of the men about German war reparations – always a good topic for anyone who fought during the war. The men were happy enough to talk about their work, although some complained that the speed of the conveyor belt made them feel like galley slaves working to the beating of a drum they could not control.[2] Drinks were bought and eventually Tom met Fred Carey, foreman of the shift.

Fred's spare angular appearance suggested he may have suffered malnutrition as a child. His impressive frame lacked substance and Tom suspected that he had tuberculosis and would eventually wither away. Even now, supposedly in his early thirties, Fred could have passed for a man 10, perhaps 15, years older.

Tom went straight to the point: "Are you good at your job, Mr Carey?"

Before the foreman could lower his pint glass and answer him, Tom added: "I need good men and I'm willing to pay above the going rate."

Fred responded: "How much?"

"What you're earning and extra."

"How much extra?"

"At least a quarter, maybe more."

"Why?"

"I'm prepared to pay good piecework rates if I can get the right men."

"How many do you need?"

"A factory full."

"Ah, the old Wheeler place? I heard someone was sniffing around there. Used to make a nice little car. When do you want them?"

"Soon, it all depends on you."

"Why me?"

Tom handed him an envelope with £20 in it: "Tomorrow is Saturday, Mr Carey. Let's meet at lunchtime and go for a little walk down to the old Wheeler place."

The next day, as Tom had hoped, it didn't take Fred long to agree in principle to the job of setting up and running the factory. Fred's eyes flickered in immediate understanding as Tom described the laundry machine. His head nodded regularly with the mental diagnoses of what was necessary to set up a production line for the machine.

"Have you being looking at Cowley and Longbridge to see how things are made, Mr Dartry?[3] Do you have any idea how many units you want to make?"

Tom was a little startled by the question. Fred continued: "It's simple. Should we sell what we can make or make what we can sell? Put another way, should your Mr Fairfax sell what suits us, or should we be flexible enough to fill the orders he gets?"

After some thought, Tom replied that the answer had to be

both. "If Mr Fairfax can't sell what we make," he explained, "or he sells what we're not making, then it's a company problem. It's a question of company policy. I'll agree a sales forecast with him and then convert it into machines, labour, money and materials. We can compare these with what we've got and then decide how much capacity to provide in the light of prices and sales. Mr Fairfax will always be worried about Albion's position in the market if we don't satisfy demand. I can see what you mean, Mr Carey: planning our manufacturing capacity now will determine our future financial results."

Tom again paused thoughtfully and then continued rather pedantically. "Mr Carey, you can assume our maximum output would be 100 units a week; I'll tell you how soon we want to reach it."

"Mr Dartry, it's not like that. Albion will be unique. We've got to cater for spares demand, seasonal fluctuations of customer demand and our ability to forecast future sales. There's a lot of it we can fix. We can hire the best foremen and managers; I can work out the production numbers for everything we make . But you've got to help, Mr Dartry. We need to know exactly how many of each type of machine you want to make each year and each week; knowing we want an average of 100 units a week is not enough."[4]

And so the conversations continued over the next fortnight until both men were mentally exhausted. By the end of Tom's second week in Mansfield, he was able to telephone James with a progress report of substance. He and Fred Carey had covered what they imagined was every possible contingency. The factory would be split in two, with the second half to be geared up for production of the Macready Mark II when it eventually was ready for manufacture. Production of Macready's first design would commence as soon as possible.

At first, the plant would need 35 men, working a single shift. Five would be needed in the motor department and another four or five making copper cylinders. Materials inspection would be necessary at the outset, but could be dispensed or reduced as time went on. Assembly would require about 10 men, with the balance acting as works engineers and office staff.

After the initial setup and teething problems, output could be expected to be over 100 units per week. Labour costs would be £400 per week, raw materials a further £670 and the value of the finished product about £5,000. On a 50-week basis, output would be valued at about a quarter of a million pounds.

Tom returned to the plant after telephoning James to find Fred standing by one of the reinforced brick walls and frowning. "This wall'll have to come down, Mr Dartry, it just disturbs the flow". Tom wondered what he meant, was Fred about to run a river through the plant?

Fred noticed Tom's frown. "I'm sorry, I forgot you've not spent your life working in a factory. You see, a plant produces thousands of the same parts which are assembled into finished goods. After a while they somehow blur together; it seems like a river passing you by. Always the same on the surface but different bits of water going past. You have to organise a factory like this too."

Tom began to listen more carefully.

"Put in too many bends and the materials get held up," Fred continued. "Leave too much empty space and it'll fill up with material like a stagnant pond. We've got to put things in straight lines; start with the goods inwards and work through to the despatch bay. These side walls just confuse things, Mr Dartry."

Tom wondered about this image of his factory and slept fitfully that night as he dreamt of Fred rowing a boat through the flooded factory singing the Eton boating song "Let's all pull together..."

Next day, Tom set off to find an electrician and plumber to form the new Works Engineering Department. He harboured doubts about Fred's picture of the factory as a river. He still saw it as something more solid – a chain, not a river.

Then it dawned on him. He and Fred were talking about the same thing. They were both looking at chains in the factory process! Now he saw the different links in the chain formed by the various departments between the suppliers and customers. For the first time, he could physically see how each depended on the other. It was no longer theory, it was reality!

The components coming into goods inwards, the castings

to the machine shop, the windings to assembly, and the laundry machines to despatch and on to the customer. The whole chain was just as strong as the weakest link. Never think you can scrimp in one area, Tom constantly repeated to himself, it'll find you out one day.

Sometimes, after work, Fred accompanied Tom back to the cottage for supper. Helen might have prepared plates of Heinz pork and beans or fish and chips which they'd eat in the kitchen or, if a fire had been prepared, in the sitting room beside the wireless. Both men, sitting with cod and chips on their laps and staring into the fire, could finally begin to relax after an 18-hour day. Fred jokingly called these events hot sweet tea talks, in reference to that beverage traditionally administered to people in shock.

During one such chat, as both men clutched their mugs of steaming tea, conversation drifted from the work that surrounded them to more theoretical matters. It soon reached the topic of the ideal factory.

"There's no such thing as an ideal factory," Fred suggested. "Every business is unique and you just can't make laundry machines in the same way you make sausages."

Fearing he might appear to be talking down to Tom, Fred guided his monologue more to Helen: "You see, there are different types of production and each affects the layout of the factory.[5] The method we're using is called flow production because all the work is done on a series of machines and flows through those machines in the same sequence. A motor car assembly line is the best example of flow production where machines might make a single standard product or more often they'll make a variety of similar products in batches but each batch follows the same sequence."

Helen interrupted Fred. "I don't understand. Do you mean all the cars coming off a production line are different?"

"They can be," he said. "Different colours, seats, engines. They don't have to be identical. What's important in flow production is that all the products flow through the machines and manual operations in the same sequence. It's generally a good idea to convert as many production stages as possible to a flow line basis."

Helen nodded in understanding and cast a glance at Tom

who by now had fallen asleep in the armchair. Fred threw a few soggy chips into the fire and, as they hissed on the coals, bade farewell and returned to his camp bed in the factory.

In the following weeks, Fred and Tom spent hours looking at sketches of material flows and trying to figure out ways to put the chain theory into practice; both men were convinced the flow of production should work, but met obstacles everywhere. Men didn't seem to know where to be or what to do.

In fact, the first half dozen washing machines that lurched off the clanging production line were unsaleable. Each had mysteriously acquired a large deep tear along one side. Tom was enraged, Fred perplexed. They soon discovered that the side panels – heavy pieces of enamelled sheet metal – were delivered in sound condition but had been gouged with meat hooks as their packing cases were grappled and lifted onto work benches. This way of handling components was dropped and replaced with a safer, if slightly more labour intensive, method.

The next 20 washing machines were produced without apparent fault. But when tested, three of the batch collapsed under the centrifugal force of the 'drying' cycle.

Tom summoned Fred to his office. Production, in his view, was in crisis. Fred nodded. The issue had suddenly become self-sufficiency or reliance on outside suppliers, who did not seem capable of producing anything of consistent quality. Tom, eyes darting across the office and onto the shopfloor, tried to control his anger: "There's nothing clever about making castings or welding steel frames. But we don't have the capital to make them ourselves, yet.[6] If we have to rely on our suppliers we have to force them to rely on us."

"I think I see what you're getting at, Mr Dartry. More chains?"

Tom now spent most of his time visiting suppliers, often playing one against the other before they could do it to him. He developed a knack for picking reliable components by following in the tracks of the car industry. The companies which were accustomed to supplying Austin, Vauxhall or Ford were more likely to be able to guarantee the quality that Tom now so desperately needed. To Tom's surprise some component manufacturers were glad to have a few tiddlers like Albion as clients, if only to allay their own fears that they were overdependent on a handful of big customers.

Tom's trusty Napier, which boasted the strongest suspension of any British car, began to show the strain of all this travelling. At times, he found himself running a virtual taxi service among suppliers and the factory, ferrying spare parts and missing tools. Occasionally, jigs and fixtures, the very backbone of engineering, would go missing and Tom would need to track them down.[7]

On one particularly successful jig-hunting expedition he failed to see a larger-than-usual pothole at the bottom of Abingdale Hill. When the weight of the solid steel slabs in the back seat was combined with the impact of the hole, the springs on the Napier broke. With the Napier off the road for a couple of weeks Tom borrowed James's Bentley, but it lacked, in Tom's eyes, the companionability of his old work horse.

On another trip through the Midlands, Tom met Frank Wollard, the manager of the vast Cowley plant. Wollard, an old acquaintance of the legendary William Morris, who by this time commanded a record half share of the whole British car market, was intrigued with Tom's chain theory of engineering. As they walked around the Cowley plant, with its thousands of workers creating an endless cacophony of terrifying sounds along miles of conveyors, Wollard cocked his ear as he listened to Tom's ambitious plans for domestic appliances.

Wollard, in turn, explained the constant commercial pressures that Morris and the company were under. He remarked how he was regularly questioned by the crusty old Morris about any plans his manager had for physical expansion of the works. And every time, he would reply there were none. "That's it my boy," Morris would shout. "Keep the walls bulging!"

A master-pupil relationship developed with Tom, who saw how Wollard's production techniques dovetailed into his own theories. Regularity in everything, Wollard urged. First achieve regularity in sales, then materials, and follow it up in quantity, quality and type. Once these have been achieved, then pursue it in workmanship and inspection.

For Tom, it was a heady cocktail of advice. He knew he could do it. With Fred and his team of workers growing in confidence every day, it was just a matter of time before they created one of the most profitable household appliance businesses in the history of Britain.

But time was not on their side.

Reference Notes

[1]Prior to the emergence of the mass car industry, cars were engineered by a host of skilled tradesmen such as coach builders, machine operators, turners, drillers, capstan gear cutters, smiths, strikers and moulders. The use of so many skilled workers, often drawn from older industries, meant that the finished product was consequently expensive. Economies of scale only became possible when mass production techniques, such as those employed on assembly lines, were introduced.

[2]A vital feature of any production line is the ability of employers to offer high rates of pay for high levels of output. The faster the parts are made or assembled, the higher the pay. Consequently, most workers like the system. One car worker in 1936 observed: "When you are on piece work, you watch the clock. You are either happy because you are in front, or you are a bit miserable because you are behind, but you are never bored."

Among the various methods of measuring piecework was the Bedaux system, under which a worker was required to produce 60 units of work an hour for a time-work rate of pay and 80 units at an incentive level of payment. On this basis the principle was established that the normal performance of time workers was three-quarters that of workers operating under incentive schemes.

[3]Continuous production flow, as developed by Henry Ford in Detroit, had only now flowered in Britain, principally again in the motor industry. By 1934, the Austin plant in Longbridge had more than 16,000 employees and boasted six miles of conveyors.

[4]Albion's quandary mirrored that of virtually every manufacturing enterprise. If a plant cannot make the volume and mix of products that its sales department sells, or if salesmen can no longer sell its output, there will be reduced revenue, lost profit and a high inventory level, all of which ultimately adversely affects a company's return on

capital employed. This problem can be minimised by advance action such as capacity planning, which strives to make available the right resources when needed.

Capacity planning takes the form of sales and production programmes which are instructions to the sales and production departments about the volume and mix of products to be made and sold in future periods. To devise these programmes, it is necessary to forecast sales opportunities, convert the sales forecast into capacity required and compare it with current capacity. Senior management can then decide if any changes should be made to capacity or the sales programme.

The meeting of the various departments involved in capacity planning, one of the key meetings held in any manufacturing business, is often called MOPS (manufacturing, operations, production and sales).

[5]Carey was alluding to the four principal methods of manufacturing – namely flow production, process production, batch production and jobbing.

Apart from flow production, which most suited the Albion plant, the other approach to large-scale production is process production. This method is employed when the same product is required all the time, as in oil refineries or chemical plants.

On a smaller scale, batch production can be employed. This method is most effective when the majority of components are standard. Drawings exist for them before a customer places an order and they are likely to have been made for stock. Components are made in batches to keep down the amount of time spent setting up machines and to increase the time actually producing. A batch may take several hours or even days to process. A skilled man will set up the machine while a semi-skilled man will operate it.

Finally, in jobbing, smaller quantities are manufactured and the variety of components produced is much greater. In batch and jobbing, it is not possible to lay out a shopfloor in a sequence of operations because there is no single sequence. There is also the tendency to employ only skilled men both for setting up the machines and processing the work.

[6]Tom Dartry quickly realised that a huge capital investment would be required if Albion were to manufacture most of its own components.

He was faced with the reality that relatively simple items such as pressed steel parts were the result of intricate and costly engineering processes.

For example, the manufacture of a pressed steel part first required a die to be designed and produced, responsibilities that fell to a factory's production engineering department. The production engineer would also fix the quantity of finished components to be stocked based on the manufacturing programme and the number required of each part. It was normal to cover a six week or three month requirement by stock though the decision in this case would be based on the manufacturing exigencies in his own factory and the time to get new supplies of raw material from other outside firms.

Before manufacture could begin, requisite tools and appliances also had to be made available. There were always innumerable small consumable tools, drills, reamers, dies, taps, files and special features such as polishing bobs and mops whose storage and supply was of considerable importance. The life of these small tools is short and often shortened by careless handling in use. There are frequent stoppages in most factories due to failure of tool supplies.

Most small tools were stocked under a 'maximum-minimum' basis. The maximum and minimum figures are based on the requirements of the machine shop and take account of the time needed to order new supplies. When the minimum level was reached a requisition for further supplies was sent to the buyer to replenish the stocks to the maximum level.

[7]For a company the size of Albion, the loss of a jig or fixture was quite a serious matter. Jigs and fixtures are used for a large percentage of the work done in machine shops and require very careful technical design and economic analysis before they are made.

The terms jig and fixture are often used interchangeably although, strictly speaking, a fixture is a work-holding device, usually secured to the table of a machine, while a jig is usually free to centre itself on the cutting tool. A fixture relies on the machine for the accuracy of the path of the cutter through the work, but in a jig the register is largely self-contained.

Wherever parts are to be produced in quantity, a certain amount of 'tooling up' is an advantage. But how far it should go and how much capital should be tied up in special fixtures and tools depends on the particular factory though such judgements are largely made even today without adequate consideration. The besetting sin of toolmakers is tying up money in fixtures which show a heavy saving in use but are seldom used. A saving of 5 per cent in the labour cost on a job in constant use might justify greater expense in fixtures than a saving of 90 per cent on a small job only coming through once or twice a year.

Most companies set guidelines that any new equipment should pay for itself in a certain period. By the 1930s, there was a wide variation in practice ranging from one to seven years, the longer period being used by railway shops, which had a stable class of work not liable to rapid obsolescence. General practice seemed to be two years.

In the early part of the decade, many engineering companies, starved of sufficient capital to replace or improve plant, were at pains to extract the maximum use out of existing equipment which in turn stifled new product development and changes in working practices.

Chapter Five – 1933

Adolf Hitler becomes Chancellor; Prohibition repealed; the
Yo-Yo; Fred Perry wins US Open; "Smoke Gets In Your Eyes"

Within three months of Albion commencing full production of its Two-in-One Laundrymatic, disaster struck. The British economy was suddenly plunged into turmoil in the wake of the stock market collapse on Wall Street in October. First to lose were the small private investors. This was followed in the second week by a further collapse in prices just as larger investors thought the market had bottomed out. In the words of one observer, the worst continued to worsen.

The 1929 crash and the economic depression that followed were, according to many subsequent US investigations, an inevitable consequence of the wild speculation in a stock market awash with liquidity.

Inevitable it may have been, but Tom along with millions others failed to recall hearing many warnings. The events of 1929 proved to be a watershed for many and for Tom it was the cruellest baptism of fire that he could have imagined.

Carey was the most bitter of all. "Nobody takes it seriously," he raged at Tom. "The root of our problem is respect. Workers don't respect owners and vice versa. In fact, many owners loathe the very factories that put bread and butter on their tables. Many don't know what goes on inside a factory and most don't care. There's fear and suspicion that factories and industry are a threat to society. Our industries are huge, enormous world leaders, but they fear they're un-English. That Fort Dunlop in Birmingham is the biggest warehouse in the world, but nobody thinks its an achievement, no they think it's a millstone. This country will never prosper if there's no regard for the factory and the factory worker."

In the recession that followed the crash, first Albion's customers began to cancel orders, then new orders became difficult to secure. One by one, Tom's suppliers were forced out of business and slowly his competitors disappeared. It was a great test of will, one which became harder each year to endure. Notwithstanding this, Tom continued to see his chains in action, but they were now shorter and more fragile than before.

By early 1933, Tom thought the worst was behind them and that some turnround was possible. Instead, he was about to receive a very nasty surprise.

Tom's real baptism of fire was about to begin when James, his fellow Signal Corps officer and business partner, now decided to abandon him – something he had never done in Flanders.

Walking into the London office on one particularly wet morning in February 1933, Tom encountered James with a facial expression almost as wretched as the weather.

"What's up, James?" Tom joked, "I'm supposed to be the miserable one around here."

"Well, old chap," James began, "I don't know quite how to break this to you but, well, I've been hankering after the life of the country squire for some time now and it would seem an opportune time to..." His voice faltered as he caught sight of the expression on Tom's face.

"You're a right bastard!" scowled Tom.

"Steady on, no need for that."

"You bastard," repeated Tom. "As soon as things get a bit tough, you bugger off – some officer you've turned out to be!" Tom was incensed at James's blatant cowardice.

"Now listen, it's not as if I didn't warn you about this," said James in his own defence. "It just happened a bit earlier than I suspected. We've been swimming against the tide for the past three years."

Tom sat slumped in his chair on his side of the desk. He kept staring at their partners' desk, such a symbol of hope in the early days, and thought how ridiculous it now looked. He was just half listening to James, catching snatches of "leave the company in your capable hands, old boy..." and "of course, will sign over rights after a few financial adjustments...". Then the awkward goodbyes and shuffling of feet.

"Bon soir, old thing," James said as he turned to go.

"Cheerio, chin, chin," Tom reluctantly replied as he stared bleakly out the window.

Chapter Five

Tom had been shell-shocked by James's decision. It mattered little that Albion was entirely his, given that most of the world was fighting for a living. His mind kept harking back to James's departure: "Bastard! He was always one for theatrics. Why couldn't he hang on a bit longer?"

Sustained only by small injections from Tom's savings – the remnants of his stock exchange bonanza in early 1929 – Albion soldiered on. One small consolation was that Empire Engineering, which had tried to run Albion out of business years earlier, was even worse off. Not quite reduced to two men and a dog, Empire was fighting for survival and, rumour had it, was teetering on the verge of bankruptcy.

Since Albion's shares were still traded on the London stock exchange, in theory it remained vulnerable to a takeover. Tom mentioned this fear to Henry Benson at Cooper Brothers. The young jocular fair-haired accountant chuckled a little to himself as he looked up the share price in *The Financial Times*: "Tuppence ha'penny? Certainly wouldn't take much to buy you out, would it? Don't worry, Tom, no one has the gumption or the money to buy Albion. We're all in the mess together."

Having been reassured that Albion was safe, Tom was more determined to make it a successful company now that James had deserted him.

By the summer of 1933, the first flickers of economic recovery were detectable and more people, donning a brittle gaiety, seemed to be singing *Happy Days Are Here Again* – the theme song of the New Deal Democrats in the US. But some of the sacrifices Tom was forced to make were more difficult than others. He temporarily abandoned Helen in the Albion cottage in Mansfield while he moved down to London to keep the Queen Street office going. He didn't like sleeping in the office but it eliminated rent and cut bus fares. Even his faithful Napier had been sold to a friend but on condition that he could buy it back should things ever improve. At weekends, it was Tom's turn to commute to the Midlands with a suitcase of laundry.

The factory he saw each weekend was a shadow of its former self; output of the Two-in-One Laundrymatic was limited to only a half dozen a week. The former workforce of 150 was reduced to 14.

In Queen Street, Tom existed on a diet of Sun-Maid raisin bread, Chiver's marmalade, Bovril and anything that caught his eye in the ABC bakery. His daily pint of milk was stored in the safe. As for business, Tom discovered that if the telephone did not ring by 11 o'clock on Monday morning, it was unlikely to ring during the rest of the week. In one bout of depression he even considered disconnecting the telephone in order to save the three shilling weekly expense of the device. Not receiving telephone calls had its positive side, of course, as it now allowed him out of the office to try to drum up some business.

In London, there were still a few affluent customers left – usually wearing last season's fashion in sympathy with the great mass of unemployed – and Tom made a point of visiting areas like Holland Park, Kensington and, if he was lucky enough to catch a Number 33 bus, to venture as far west as Richmond. But even these well-heeled markets were thinning and Tom knew he would have to rethink his whole business approach.

One evening, alone in Queen Street, Tom propped his feet up on the partners' desk, poured a large whisky – he had set aside a bottle of his favourite Vat 69 for such emergencies – lit a pipe and stared at one of the laundry machines standing in the middle of the room. It conjured up uncomfortable memories of their demonstration to City investors five years previously.

The laundry machine cast a long shadow, perhaps distorted by the alcohol, and increasingly looked like an automaton from an H. G. Wells novel. It could have been a cosmic shape from another world – wires hung from the back while copper sheeting, still retaining its reddish hue, caught the moonlight. Tom looked at the austere figure in front of him and no longer viewed it as a single unified machine.

Slowly, he examined each part of the machine at a distance. Then he approached it and using whatever tools or brute force were necessary removed the components from the machine. In turn, he stared at each of the parts and tried to think of alternative uses.

The broad principle of a rotating vessel that heated or dried the contents had a limited number of applications. He had already approached Baker Perkins, the food equipment maker, about using his machine for bread or confectionery manufacturing, but their own engineers were already developing new dough mixing machines. Pinchin Johnson, the coatings company, had expressed some interest in the idea of treating special varnishes for marine use, but it was doubtful whether the mixer could be upgraded to produce higher temperatures and greater control over heat dissipation. Tom was now discovering that hopping from one market to another did not necessarily work. He thought about applications in the building trade, perhaps as a mobile cement mixer, but couldn't see any market potential for it.

By the end of a half bottle of whisky, he could list four possible uses for the copper cylinders but perhaps a dozen for the electric motors.

Motors, more expensive and more complicated than copper cylinders, were easier to manufacture because they lent themselves to assembly line conditions. Each function could be broken down into many simpler operations. It was no single flash in the pan that produced this product but rather a steady accumulation of skilled and semi-skilled actions. Henry Ford's techniques had already been shown to work in Albion's own humble factory. In fact, Macready – that stalwart boffin who was hanging on by a thread with a few others in Mansfield – had managed to tinker with his original motor so much that it now no longer resembled the first design he had developed in 1929. What Tom now had was a motor that could be run at a highly accurate rate of revolutions per minute and which did not burn out as quickly as other motors. In an effort to cut down on waste, Macready had even decided to make it smaller by having the parts finely machined and then assembled by two young teenage girls, whose manual dexterity surpassed any male colleague.

As Tom dozed off in his chair, he tried one last time to think of how his engineering chains might help them.

The following morning, a cloud of fine dust whirled into the office as Tom let the roller blinds spin out of control and sunlight hesitantly peaked through the elaborate italic name on the window.

It was time to change tactics, Tom concluded as he boiled a kettle for his breakfast. Ideas about chains were fine, but he realised he had to put them into practice. At the moment sales were virtually non-existent simply because people could not afford his washing machines. The critical links in the chain were broken and he had to repair them somehow.

Instead of looking for outright purchases, he now adopted the principle of hire-purchase, where the customer paid a small initial deposit and bought the item over a fixed number of instalments. By following other consumer appliance manufacturers down this route, Tom was able to reach a wider market of potential customers that had not existed for him. Once he started to sell some of the huge stockpile of laundry machines in the Old Kent Road warehouses, he began to generate a reliable cash flow for the first time in years.

Fortunately great care had been taken in storing the finished units. Most of the machines, which had nickel-plated components as well as enamelled sides, were draped with canvas covers to keep them free of dust and too much light. Even though stored for months, the washing machines were in pristine condition.

The warehouse in the Old Kent Road was a remarkable place, with rows and rows of sheeted machines. Most of the money in Albion was tied up in these finished machines. Withdrawals from the store were handled very carefully to avoid fraud and could only be done by Tom or the sales representative before he was laid off. Unlike the rest of the works withdrawals were done by quoting catalogue not part numbers. At the end of each month the stocks were balanced by recording all issues and receipts. As he also knew the monthly manufacturing schedule in the event that stocks were running low, Tom could see what was in the process of manufacture and when it could be expected to be delivered.

Tom considered his next decision a minor masterstroke. With the concept of the chains still firmly fixed in his mind, he hired a plumber. He now offered the services of this tradesman at half the normal rate and with the guarantee that the washing machine would be installed on the day of delivery. Within weeks, Tom's plumber became so adept at installations he could fit the machine in less than an hour. The chain was strengthened because Albion knew its product was functioning properly.

Chapter Five

As the stocks of washing machines dwindled in number and the precarious finances of the company steadied, Tom announced he was closing the factory. For a fortnight!

For the first time in four years, the remnants of the Albion workforce were given a paid holiday. Helen set off with ten employees, some with spouses and girlfriends, on a hiking holiday on the Continent, a trip arranged through the aptly-named International Tramping Tours. Tom treated himself by dropping into Keith Prowse and booking the best seat he could get for the touring Swedish ballet in the Palace Theatre. En route to the theatre he paid a visit to Austin Reed in nearby Cheapside and was measured for a new suit. With a flourish of opulence more reminiscent of James Fairfax, he selected three fabrics, each a little more daring than the previous.

While Helen and most of the company were trekking across the Continent, a more confident and certainly better dressed Tom Dartry received a telephone call one Monday morning from an RAF officer. It proved to have far-ranging implications.

The officer had spotted one of Albion's laundry machines in the Royal Artillery kitchens the previous year and had now decided to buy one as an anniversary gift for his wife. When Tom arrived in South Kensington with the machine the following afternoon he received a warm welcome.

"Dapper piece of work, Mr Dartry. What else do you make?"

"We were working on a wider range of washers and dryers but we've had to postpone some of our development," Tom said grandly.

"Research and development, Mr Dartry, very important. New ideas are needed all the time. Take the Royal Air Force, for example. We're keen to make up lost ground and we're looking for new concepts to help us."

Tom exchanged cards with the officer, but expected little to come of the gesture.

Several weeks later, at about 10.00 on Monday morning, the telephone rang. A man named Ridgewater from the Air Ministry claimed he had been trying to telephone all the previous week. He wanted to meet Tom to discuss the purchase of some of his products.

51

An invitation from the Air Ministry to talk about laundry machines? Tom was perplexed. None the less at the appointed hour, he presented himself in an obscure building in Whitehall. Armed with several brochures and a few sketches of new ideas that Macready had drafted, he sallied forth.

It was a dismal affair. Conditions of secrecy were insisted upon, meticulous notes were made by a stenographer, public records of his company were examined in fine detail, and he was constantly under the stern gaze of two officers who remained silent throughout the interview, which was taking on the tone of an interrogation.

His feelings of being held prisoner were heightened when he was questioned about his customers. Who they were, how many foreign nationals bought the machines, did he export them, if so, where? He felt like he was being dragged slowly through a wringer. When he caught sight of files on Chelmsford Founders and Empire Engineering on the desk in front of him, he grinned at the thought of his competitors having to go through the same indignities.

"We have assumed the machines have operated under normal atmospheric conditions only," said the sole officer with the gift of speech.

"Errh? Yes." Tom shifted uneasily in his chair.

"If we wanted a large order, perhaps with design alterations, could you produce them?"

"Altered in what way?" Tom was becoming a little wary of this chap opposite him.

"We don't know yet. We want to test some of them first," the officer responded with a casual shake of his head. "Can you handle design modifications?"

"Albion has one of the best engineering designers alive," Tom countered. "We can make anything you need."

Dazed after his three-hour interrogation, Tom walked out into the cold grey daylight, only partially content with an order for three laundry machines.

Two weeks later Tom was summoned to a well-maintained military compound in Acton in west London. He was greeted by a single officer, who dispensed with most military formality and poured numerous cups of tea for his civilian guest. Munching on a plain biscuit, he explained to Tom that all incoming equipment was tested against a number of critical factors and that Albion's had done quite well on most of them. The officer smiled.

"What about price?" asked Tom.

"No, we're more interested in reliability and adaptability. Size is also quite important. Price only becomes a factor later. We're more interested in what machines like yours can do. But we may need to look more closely at a few details." Tom was then invited to accompany the officer to another part of the barracks.

Tom's stomach churned as they began a long walk across the parade yard. He tried to explain to the officer his approach to manufacturing and how he saw things from strategic and tactical perspectives.

"Hmmmm. Interesting," his escort replied as they entered a small hangar, stuffed full of crates and mounds of scrap metal. The officer excused himself and asked Tom to wait a few minutes.

More akin to a junk yard than a military establishment, the hangar exuded an aura of decay and demise. Tom noticed a fire engine reel in one corner, a smart looking Bedford lorry and some coils of cabling left in a pile in the middle of the floor. A work bench with oil-stained chairs on either side occupied one wall.

Tom made for a chair and sat down. He lit his pipe. His eyes wandered around the hangar again and returned to the bench beside him. Tea chests choked full of debris were stored under the bench and stacked along the side walls. He scanned the boxes and suddenly focused on the name *Albion Engineering*.

He pulled the cover off the box. Slowly he recognised a part, a couple of wing nuts, a bit of metal housing. The mangled contents were, in fact, part of one of his washing machines. He was still in a state of near-shock when a voice whispered in his ear: "Our tests are quite comprehensive."

Tom jumped back to see the officer standing beside him again.

"Do you have to test them until they fall apart?" he asked, but regretted it almost as soon as he said it.

"Oh yes; this one over here is quite a treasure. It doesn't

look like it, but it still works – barely. It was salvaged from a crashed aircraft. Quite good; I was impressed with it but not with the aeroplane. We've tinkered around with some of the configurations over here."

They walked over to another bench, and the officer pulled back a tarpaulin. Tom tried to recognise his laundry machine – normally in the shape of a two foot cube on legs – but couldn't. He saw some of Macready's components, but the shape had either been flattened or rounded.

"We had to cut up one of the motors to see how it performed and X-rayed the other after it went through the tests, Mr Dartry. It's hard to replicate battlefield conditions and then accelerate the process. But on the whole you have some very fine motors which appeal to us."

"Motors? I thought you wanted my laundry machines."

The officer laughed quietly to himself. "Your laundry machines are splendid devices, but we're only interested in the motors. Washing laundry is not a problem for us, but finding a high-powered compact motor that can operate in tough conditions had been."

Tom looked confused.

"Mr Dartry, you mentioned strategy and tactics on your way here. Your motors may have a strategic advantage that we desperately need. They're more reliable, smaller and quieter than anything else we've found. Now Mr Dartry, you'll have to start thinking tactically about how many of these you can produce."

The two men left the hangar and walked across the muddied courtyard to a grey stone building where Tom was given a detailed explanation of how Ministry contracts operated. Various proposals were put to Tom whereby output of the factory would be altered and a monthly order for 250 motors would be placed. He could continue to manufacture his laundry machines, if he liked, but production of the motors would now be deemed a military matter. Sales records, he was informed, would have to be examined, particularly any exports to Germany or Austria. Any future exports would be monitored and only under special circumstances would exports to possible belligerents be permitted. Tom protested at this restriction on a mere laundry machine, but was firmly told that he had no choice in the matter. Others might spot the capabilities of the motor, just as they had. It was something they could not risk.

Although it was never actually mentioned, Tom was left in no doubt that Albion, and his engineering chains, were preparing for war.

The Air Ministry contract was a life saver. Tom quickly set up a planning session, first with Fred over immediate production and then with Macready over development of the motors.

Within the Albion factory, some of the old internal walls, demolished years earlier, were rebuilt as safety precautions and a portion of the factory was dedicated solely to motor output. For Tom and Fred, it was a clear signal that the chains running through the company were changing shape.

Fred had relished the prospect of trying something new – of setting up an entire factory-within-a-factory, exclusively for production of the military motors. Chains within chains. He found, however, that the flow of materials, and the men pursuing them to make the laundry machines, lacked the adaptability that was needed. He found that if he wanted his factory-within-a-factory he would need to install production equipment solely for this output. On the strength of the Ministry orders, Tom secured a further £10,000 loan to buy the necessary machine tools for the new production.

Fred's factory-in-a-factory concept would prove to be only a temporary experiment since the steady increase of Ministry orders in the following years would force Albion to dedicate virtually its entire production to military output. However, as an idea, he would muse in years to come, it still had a lot of appeal.

Meanwhile, Macready set to developing new and better motors. But not before the crusty 57-year-old boffin had married Helen's mother and, in a loose sense, had become Tom's father-in-law.

Macready now concentrated his research efforts in a cold laboratory and spartan office once again located on the second floor. The lab, with moisture-laden windows, was as cold as a morgue and anyone brave enough to visit would need to don extra layers of clothing.

Inside his miniature office – tucked away in a corner of the lab – pride of place had been given to his antiquated drafts- man's table, locked in the horizontal position and piled high with paper and suppliers' handbooks.[1] His favourite was a small well-thumbed 800-page blue book called *A Pocket Book for Mechanical Engineers* by Professor D. A. Low. Beside the draftsman's table was a well-scrubbed wooden kitchen table, with a kettle, a cluster of dirty chipped teacups, a packet of Tate & Lyle sugar and a makeshift ashtray, which Macready had fashioned out of up-ended pistons. This ashtray, over- flowing with Woodbine butts, competed with some scribbled pencil notes and an ivory and wooden slide rule for the remaining space.

Macready was an empirical designer. He would say that theory was fine, but it rarely led to new ideas. Tom half suspected that the limit of Macready's theoretical knowledge was to calculate the number of windings needed in a partic- ular coil. However, when it came to making things Macready was pure genius. A steady stream of radical new motor designs, often backed up with full working models, came out of the lab.

With Albion's fortunes beginning to recover, it was only a matter of time before the financial press noticed. In turn, the stock market responded and Albion's share price staged a remarkable recovery.

By the summer of 1934, Tom sensed that things were looking brighter. If he needed any confirmation of this renais- sance of the English spirit after years of misery, he only had to look as far as Wimbledon where the tennis championships were underway. Miraculously, for the first time in 25 years, Wimbledon produced English champions. Fred Perry won the men's singles title and Dorothy Round the women's title. It was a glorious 6-3, 6-0, 7-5 victory for Perry. Tom was not on hand to view this moment in history. Instead, he was stuck in an Underground tunnel on the District Line for the entire match. Now every time he heard the names Perry or Wimbledon, Tom scowled. Maybe next year, he thought.

Equally out of the blue, he met James Fairfax again. One Saturday afternoon, as Tom was walking around the Mansfield factory floor checking machinery and stores, he heard a rat-tat-tat on the half-open steel main door. In walked James. The two men had not seen each other for 18 months. Each, unsure of the other's reaction, stared for a moment and then warmly shook hands.

"Helen said you were here," James began, looking around the assembly floor and glancing at Tom's well-cut suit. "It looks like you saved the lot. How did you do it?"

"With a lot of luck and, maybe, my chains," Tom remarked impishly.

"You and your chains!" James threw his hands into the air.

"We needed you here, James, there was so much to be done." Tom paused a moment and then asked what his former partner had done in the past 18 months.

"Oh, you know, bits and pieces. Some import, some export. I travel a great deal. Mostly to eastern Europe. Exotic places like Prague, Berlin and Moscow. It's amazing what you find in these out-of-the-way places."

"Why didn't you stay a bit longer, help me see it through?" Tom almost regretted blurting this out but James quickly saved him any embarrassment.

"Oh, Tom, old boy, I would have loved that, but I was bored with laundry machines and quickly became bored living the life of a squire. Once I'd done these, I wanted bigger challenges. I even did something patriotic. By the way, did an RAF bod from South Kensington ever contact you?" asked James with a twinkle in his eye.

Light dawned in Tom's eyes as he understood the significance of what James had just said. "I wondered how they found my name! You really are a Svengali."

James took the remark as a compliment but then turned sombre. He explained that since they last saw each other, James had married. Tom's eyes sparkled with the news. But James continued in a subdued monotone: it had been a whirlwind romance in eastern Europe, a few months of married bliss, then a baby, a son in fact, and suddenly his wife died of cholera.

Tom was crest-fallen and didn't know whether to reply.

"The boy is fine. Anthony Thomas Fairfax!" James now thundered. "Born in a good hotel in Lithuania while his father sold machine tools to the Soviets. His mother was a beauty, a real beauty. I want you and Helen to be his godparents. I want him to have some roots in this country."

Tom's eyes sparkled again and a broad grin erupted on his face. Of course they would.

"Good!" James said with the air of an impresario. "With that settled, show me what you and Fred have done to dear old Albion. And don't start on again about these blasted chains!"

Chapter Notes

The 1929 stock market crash, with the financial ruin that ensued for many private investors, was reminiscent of the great South Sea Bubble disaster on the London Stock Exchange in the 1720s. However, this twentieth-century financial catastrophe was more notable in that it engendered world economic depression on a scale never before imagined.

In due course, the British government, when faced with three million people out of work, was forced initially to abandon its free trade policy and later its support of the gold standard. Many attempts to stimulate the economy, which remained firmly rooted in depression for the early part of the decade, proved inadequate. One such policy was to cut the cost of borrowing in the hope that economic regeneration would follow.

In fact, the 1930s would be the age of cheap money as witnessed by the fact that the Bank of England discount rate was held at 2 per cent from 1932 to 1939.

This cheap source of financing in time lead to a housing boom and the construction of almost three million new dwellings, twice as many as during the 1920s. Such new housing led to the development of London's girdle of middle-class suburbs and in turn fuelled the demand for new innovative electrical appliances, such as cookers, radios and phonographs.

Mechanical and electrical engineering industries benefited enormously from this new source of demand. By the end of the decade, a further one million motor vehicles joined the existing 1.5 million vehicles already on British roads. The motor car industry was a huge consumer of semi-finished and finished intermediate products (such as sheet steel, timber, glass and paint) and components (tyres, lamps and generators). In 1936, the British motor vehicle industry consumed 900,000 tons of iron and steel – 8.2 per cent of total national output.

The real driving force behind the British economic recovery, however, was the decision to re-equip the armed forces in the light of German military expansion. In November 1933, Stanley Baldwin, soon to be prime minister for the third time, announced plans to strengthen Britain's armed forces, after other countries had failed to follow Britain's earlier lead in disarmament. Over the next six years, major efforts were made to strengthen the Royal Air Force and increase the number of its military aircraft to levels comparable to France, Italy and the US.

Such an expansive rearmament programme had a direct impact on the economic fortunes of many engineering and strategic commodity producers. By the end of the 1930s, a large number of London stock market shares, loosely termed War Stocks, benefited from strong buying. Companies producing automobiles, engineering products, petroleum products, and rubber were all considered to have good commercial prospects in the event of war.

In the event, by 1939, Britain was spending a higher proportion of its GNP on arms production than Germany.

Reference Notes
[1]For designers like Macready, suppliers' handbooks are the stock in trade. They contain empirical or experimental results which enable the designer, having specified a physical characteristic such as voltage, power/air flow, etc., to select the manufacturers' product which will provide that effect. These handbooks often contain information of a more fundamental nature such as steam tables, expansion coefficients of various alloys or electrical resistance of different conductors. The extent to which such reference materials are used by designers is of considerable concern as they can lead to over-engineering, parts proliferation and increased product cost.

Chapter Six – 1939

Poland invaded; Royal Oak torpedoed in Scapa Flow; income tax jumps to 35%; "Over The Rainbow"

"You lot have been trading on the name of British industry too long," the officer bellowed at the small gathering. "We want something like your grandfathers were making. Quality! Lots of it, and cheap. Our lives depend on it!"

Within days of war being declared in September 1939, Tom, along with the heads of several dozen other small engineering firms, was summoned to a special meeting outside London organised by the newly formed Ministry of Supply. Top of the agenda was getting the firms to double their production as rapidly as possible.

In front of him, an overweight officer marched up and down the small stage in the Ealing school hall. Tom suspected he might have been a bank manager in his former life.

"Any of you who care to remember the last war will recall one word. 'Obsolete'. The horse and cart became obsolete; carrier pigeons were obsolete. We finished with tanks, lorries, aircraft and machine guns. The end was totally different from the beginning. The same will happen this time, only our starting point is so much further ahead. So if you've got ideas, you'd better get working on them now. They'll be needed sooner than you think."

Perhaps an accountant? Tom thought.

"One thing is certain. We will finish the war with something we never thought possible." He paused briefly for breath. "Hopefully, it will not be another fight to the finish in trenches, but a more civilised way of dealing with the enemy. Now, how many of you have done government work before?"

A few hands were raised.

"You will remember how difficult it was to have a contract signed."

A few heads nodded. Tom recalled his first introduction to military procurement six years earlier and how Albion, almost on the point of extinction, had been saved by the timely arrival of an Air Ministry order. Tom chuckled to himself how naive he had been in thinking the Royal Air Force wanted to buy his washing machines, when in fact they were really interested in Macready's motors.

Out of curiosity, shortly after receiving his first order from the Ministry, Tom had paid a surprise visit to Arthur Woods, head of arch competitor Empire Engineering. As he suspected, he saw the same buzz of activity in Empire's assembly hall. The company appeared to have been saved by military contracts too – although neither mentioned it.

Now sitting in the Ealing school hall, he caught sight of Woods – looking in need of a shave although it was barely lunchtime – trying to stay awake during the lecture.

The well-fed officer descended into a monotonous pep-talk: "We're gathered here to improve the performance of all your factories.[1] We don't care if you compete against each other but, gentlemen, remember the real competition at the moment is Germany."

Tom began to wonder where the talk was heading.

"You must optimise production," the uniformed lecturer announced, "because you are all using too many short runs. Machines are idle because of frequent set-ups and workers don't have the chance to acquire skill and speed in any one operation. The Production Efficiency Board has been set up to overcome permanently the ineffectiveness of haphazard methods of training. You must use it if you want to get more orders."

The officer paused briefly and continued with a flourish and a wave of his hands in the air for dramatic effect: "*If* management fails to standardise component parts, further waste takes place."

Again, with emphasis on the "*if*", he began to get his audience's attention:

"*If* component designs are changed while the parts are in the course of production, you will have lost working time and materials because 'old' parts have to be swapped for new.

"*If* management fails to ensure raw materials and tools are in place to do the work, more time is lost.

"*If* you don't maintain your plant and machines in good

working order, your production will be crippled by breakdowns.

"It may be strategically important to manufacture two-inch diameter ball bearings instead of one-inch bearings. That's our decision. You lot just keep churning them out."

Tom ears suddenly jumped when he heard the word *strategic.*

"You decide how best to use your resources and make as many of those bearings as possible. After you've been making them for a while, you should be able to make them better and cheaper. If they are shot out of the sky, we want to be able to salvage them and use them again." Now puffing with excitement, he declared: "We don't want the junk you normally make."

Tom glanced across at Arthur Woods who had woken up.

"Remember, we do things one way in peacetime and another way in war," the officer continued. "Once the shooting starts, things change quite quickly. We make up our minds and stick with it. But there's another big difference.

"In quieter times, you're the ones knocking on our door looking for new orders. Now, we're hammering on your door, telling you we want something made quickly and showing you some ways to do it.

"Remember, without proper design, it will be impossible to manufacture properly. Clarity of thought, singularity of purpose; with these you win wars and you might learn something about manufacturing also."

The officer was given a polite round of applause which was quickly drowned by the shifting of chairs and a general rush for the door. In the crush near the exit, Tom reluctantly found himself pressed arm to arm against Arthur Woods.

"I hear you're making 750 a week," Woods said baldly.

"750 what?"

An exasperated Woods turned on Tom: "Motors, damnit!"

"Arthur, who fills your head with this nonsense. We're doing well, but not that well.

Woods persisted: "What's all this about chains and your chain gang?"

"That's just a little joke in the works. I must tell you about it sometime." Tom tried to change the subject. "What do you think about this ministerial directive?"

"You mean about productivity? Pie in the sky, if you ask me. I've heard of wishful thinking, but I don't see how anyone could double output in three months. We'll all try of course, but so long as we stick together, they can't penalise us."

"I'm certain we'll all do our best, Arthur. Take care, I've got to dash back to Mansfield now." Tom bade farewell to Woods and headed for his car, which he had parked carefully beside an officer's green Vauxhall outside the town hall. As he climbed into the Napier – the very same car he had reluctantly parted with five years earlier but had since repurchased – Tom thought what the odds were against doubling their production in three months. For the most part of the three-hour journey back to Mansfield, he toyed with what might have to be done to his company to achieve such a phenomenal jump in output.

When Tom coasted the last 15 yards into the gravel driveway outside the Mansfield factory later that afternoon, he sensed something was wrong. In blatant violation of the blackout rules, lights burned brightly in the front offices, yet the factory was deadly quiet. As he headed through the main works entrance, he was confronted by a small knot of people with Fred in the middle.

Fred was the first to talk. Three of their best engineers – the men standing around Fred – were leaving, he was told. Or more correctly, they were being redeployed with ministerial approval, to work for Empire Engineering.

"The lads were told to be ready to leave on Friday, to head down to London where they were really needed. I got a telephone call from a Ministry official who said I'd be next. He said rumours were that I was responsible for increasing output. Well, I told him I'd rather shoot myself than work for Empire and he could put that in his despatches!"

"Don't worry, Fred, you're not going anywhere," Tom said with as much reassurance as he could cram into his voice but was almost immediately interrupted by the sound of a low-flying aircraft. Everyone looked toward the skylights and listened for a moment.

"As for you three, I'll do everything to stop the transfer or to get you back as soon as possible. Even if it means doubling production! We still have a few days to work out something.

Now off you go and don't worry the rest of the men. No one is being forced to leave Albion."

As soon as they left, Tom sat down again and stared his works manager in the face. "How do we do it, Fred? How do we show them that we're the best and if they want the maximum out of us, they must leave us alone?"

"It's easier than you think, Mr Dartry. Let's put these chains to work. If they want motors, let's give them as many as we can. We can frighten them with our production. They'll be afraid to come poaching again, and it'll warn Arthur Woods to keep his nose out of our business."

The fighter aircraft returned and a few seconds later was followed by another in pursuit.

"My god, this really is war. We'll beat Hitler, Fred, but we'll also teach Empire Engineering a lesson about stealing our men."

Fred almost snapped to attention. "Bravo, Mr Dartry. So what's our plan?"

"You mean the strategy and tactics."

Fred looked a little admonished. "Of course, I almost forgot."

"The Ministry must already know our production is crucial! We'll show them how important those three men are to us. What we need is a sudden jump in output and if the three lads are taken from us, output falls back. They'll take note of that.

"Then we show them our plans for raising output by one-third in the next month and doubling it within six months. But only on condition that they leave us with our engineering staff. This will be so far ahead of anything Empire or Chelmsford can offer, they'll leave us alone. Later we'll offer to show them some of our working practices, but maybe we'll leave out the theory." Looking Fred straight in the face, Tom asked how many motors could be made by Friday.

"Well, last week we made 770." Fred wrinkled his nose, frowned slightly and offered: " Why not 1,000?"

"If you think it can be done, let's talk to the men and check the supplies."

Fred sounded the shop floor whistle. Apart from signalling breaks and the end of shifts, it was rarely used. He asked the shift foreman to assemble the men in the canteen, while he carried out a swift survey of goods inwards, work in progress and stock levels.

Grinning to himself, Fred appeared a few minutes later and told the men that Mr Dartry had something important to tell them. It was something that would affect everyone. A ripple of unease passed through the hundred odd men crammed into the canteen.

"Here he comes, men. A bit of hush, please."

Tom Dartry stood at the end of the canteen, flanked by a large milk churn and several crates of apples.

"I'm sorry to drag you away from your work," Tom started. "But I have something important to tell you. This afternoon I discovered some of our men are to be sent to other factories to help them with their production. In other circumstances, this would be a compliment. But we're at war now and we have a big job ahead of us. Some of you will want to leave us for the army anyway. Others will want to work here as long as possible. In the meantime, I need every man I can keep."

A few mutters of approval came from the back.

"I need every man because this week Mr Carey and I are going to increase output by one third. By 6 o'clock on Friday!"

An audible gasp was heard from the middle of the canteen.

" I don't know how we're going to do it," Tom continued, "but if we succeed, we'll be able to show these people in Whitehall that Mansfield men work best when left alone."

A fitter in the front shouted "Hear, Hear".

"If we succeed, Bill Kerridge, Harry Blackwell and John Evans here might not have to leave us. Albion will be a safer place for all to work in."

A man from the back of the canteen shouted: "Three cheers for Mr Dartry" and the rest of the men shouted a trio of Hip, Hip, Hurrays.

Fred moved forward. "Men, I'm looking for 1,000 motors by close of business on Friday. It's Tuesday afternoon and we've done 180." He shuffled a little uneasily. "There's enough materials for another 800, so I'll get more by tomorrow. When the night shift comes in, they'll be asked to do the same. We need a one-week wonder to save our jobs.

Next week, we'll see how we can make another 1,000 but without all this heartache. Let's do it for Bill, Harry and Jack."

The canteen reverberated with loud cheers again and then there was a mad scramble for the doors leading to the assembly works.

Fred returned to his office. He looked out the window at the light rain that was beginning to fall. How do we do it? he quietly questioned himself.

"Honest hard work," said a voice from behind him. Tom was standing in the doorway. "Let's see how many we need at the end of each day," Tom suggested. "Then we show the men the actual production against the target output. We need to remind them how important each link in the production chain is. Fred, we can do it! I know we can!"

Tom now instructed Fred to select a different man to help him each day. Simple jobs, like seeing that the castings were coming out on time, and that fettling was up to scratch before the finishing. At the end of the day, this man would know more about the chain than ever before.

"When we reach the 500th motor," Tom told Fred, "we stop for an extra tea break. Shut the plant down for 15 minutes. Do the same when we reach 750. After another 100 or so, tell the men there'll be extra in their paypacket and that the drinks are on you at the Pig & Whistle at a half past six on Friday."

As Fred was making notes of Tom's instructions, Macready stuck his head into the office. "I've been looking for you, Mr Carey," he said innocently.

"Samuel Macready!" Tom declared with gusto. "What a surprise. You're just the man we need."

"I wanted to ask you about one of the new motor designs," Macready began.

"Sam, hang new motors this week," Tom interrupted, "we're making 1,000 of the best motors in production, and you're going to help us."

"Me, but I know nothing about a production line."

"You took the words out of my mouth, Sam. You're going to learn everything there is to know about a production line by asking each man how you can make his job easier."

"Me?" Macready's face contorted in disbelief and then turned to mild horror when he realised that Tom was serious. "Me?"

"Sam, they love you already. They'll love you all the more if you give them an easier motor to make. Talk to them."

Macready shuffled uneasily back to his lab, still in a state of shock.

The remainder of the week was like a relay race. The plant was never idle. Fred was always on the move, trying to unclog bottlenecks and sort out small irritations. Fresh materials arrived and were promptly pushed into the system.

By late Wednesday, 500 motors had been made. Fred was on hand as this milestone motor was hoisted off the production line, tested and approved by the works electrical engineer, who was now helping in quality control. A group of men gathered around the motor and Fred produced a small pot of silver paint – the type that garden railings are painted with. Inside the motor's cowling, Fred carefully painted the number 500 and the date to commemorate the event. "Right lads, we're stopping for quarter of an hour. Enjoy the break."

A scene more common in school yards developed. Oily rags, wing-nuts and wire cabling suddenly shot into the air. School was out and the night shift at Albion were enjoying themselves and celebrating a small victory. Now for the next 500!

The mood in the works and the cottage was one of spirited resistance. Helen joined in the effort by baking two dozen apple pies – Tom couldn't stand the smell of baking apples for months afterward – and gave them to the canteen staff to distribute among the men during their break. And as a special treat, Tom also tracked down several large tins of scarce Kit-Kats.

Amid the hub-bub, Tom began thinking about the following week's production. It would probably fall back to 750, making an average of 875 a week if they managed to produce 1,000 this week. He decided he'd recommend to war production officials that a weekly goal of 1,500 could be attained in his factory faster than anywhere else.

But for the moment, it was a case of all hands to the pump.

By Thursday night, a bleary-eyed Fred – who had been roused from his canvas camp bed in his office – appeared on the production line to welcome the 750th completed motor. A quick test by the electrician assured everyone that it was in sound working order and Fred ceremoniously painted '750' and the date in large silver numerals. To everyone's surprise, he pulled a football rattle out of his pocket, clacked it around his head several times and announced another celebratory halt.

By now fatigue was beginning to show in the men. The few oily rags that were thrown into the air didn't reach the same height as Wednesday night. Instead the men, sat on crates and joked for a while. A few went outside for a smoke.

At 6.30 the following morning, Fred had breakfast in the Dartry cottage. Sitting opposite Helen and Tom, and looking unshaven and a little wild-eyed, Fred prepared to give his progress report.

"Would you like some more tea, Mr Carey?" Helen enquired sympathetically.

Still somewhat dazed from lack of sleep, Fred was slow to respond. "Eh? No, thank you, Mrs Dartry, I'm fine for now."

Tom asked about the night shift's output.

"We're doing very well, Mr Dartry, a total 790 by the end of the shift this morning. Only another 210 to go."

Today was their last day of production. "Will we make it?" Tom asked eagerly.

"I don't know," Fred said honestly. "Everyone's done so well but they're near the end of their rope. We might be able to do another 160 or 170 today."

As Helen started to clear away the breakfast dishes, she heard her six-month-old son George crying in the adjoining room. She suspected three-year-old James was banging something against his younger brother's cot again. Her first son had been named, somewhat generously in her eyes, after Tom's ex-business partner who had absconded in the middle of the Depression. But when it came to naming their second son, she was adamant that he be named after the late King George. Now, having spent most of the night awake with the infant, Helen was insistent that George be left to sleep.

Back in the kitchen, Tom scraped a bit of butter on his toast and looked earnestly at Fred and asked what could give them the extra push they needed.

"I don't rightly know," said Fred. "Macready certainly helped their spirits. He lifted them a bit, you know. Maybe you..."

Chapter Six

"I understand, Fred," Tom had made up his mind. "Find a pair of overalls for me. I'll change when I get over there. We've got to strengthen the chain."

The Albion day shift was gob-smacked when they saw Tom Dartry in blue engineers' overalls walking down the assembly hall. Word spread quickly.

"Morning, Joe," Tom said as he passed one of his men.

A dumbfounded Joe Malone, long accustomed to seeing Fred Carey walking up and down the production line, could barely reply when he realised the figure in overalls was in fact the head of the entire company. The best he could muster was a meek "Morning, Mr Dartry."

Tom put himself under Fred's direction for the entire day. When Fred needed a barrow full of castings, he asked Tom and another man, who by this stage had an impish grin on his face, to fetch them.

"It's good to see you here, Mr Dartry," said one fitter as they pushed the barrow along.

"Glad to be here, Mike. How's the wife?"

"Bit of a cold at the moment, but should be fine in a few days."

"Send her my regards," groaned Tom as they pushed the barrow over a small ramp in the factory.

"I'll do that, Mr Dartry, you can rely on me."

The oil-stained hands, cut thumb and aching back that Tom earned that day did the trick. Like the cavalry riding to the rescue in a Hollywood film, Tom's presence helped the day shift at Albion to soldier on. Their spirit was galvanised.

At lunchtime, Tom stood in the line at the canteen with his tray like the other 103 men. A few may have noticed the extra large portion of mashed potato given to Tom but no mention was made of it.

Tom sat with the three men he had been helping just before the whistle. Conversation revolved around the blackout, football, and reports that women were going to get the same rate of pay as men. Tom tried to keep pace with some of the names of footballers but could only claim that none of them seemed a match for Ben Kiley of Wolverhampton. The whistle blew sooner than Tom would have liked but with the rest of the weary shift he returned to his place on the production line.

Within a few minutes, he was manhandling castings onto trolleys and filling up wire baskets with gaskets. Fred called him over and said he wanted a word with him in the office. As Tom closed the door, Fred asked how he was feeling.

"A bit of a sore back, but otherwise alright. How are we doing?"

"We've done 944," Fred started to scribble with a pencil on a flattened cigarette pack. "There's four hours to make 56. That's a rate of 14 an hour. I think we're going to make it."

Tom now told Fred to pass the word along when they reached 950. "And let them know when the next 10 is complete and the 10 after that. The production chain will hold fast as long as we keep telling them how well they're doing." Tom then walked back to his place on the production line.

As instructed, Fred clocked in the completion of each 10 new motors. He toyed with the idea of a football or cricket scoreboard to pass the news to the men, but knew time was against him. Instead Tom Franklin, the works electrical engineer, shouted out the numbers to him after he tested them. Like a railway guard shouting the departure of the 11.47 to Crewe, Fred blew his whistle and bellowed the numbers to the entire works:

"...960 ... 970 ... 980 ... 990 ... 995 ... 999..."

At 10 minutes to six, a hush fell over the Albion plant. The foundry had finished their last castings, the fettling shop had been abandoned and the stores appeared as empty as a toy shop the day after Christmas. The entire workforce had gathered at one end of the factory.

There, on a small table, stood a motor. No different to the thousands of motors that had been made in the factory over the years. But this one had a special pride of place in the hearts and minds of the men who had made it. It was the 1,000th motor to be made that week. Now all that was needed was for the electrician to give it a final test and it would be accepted into the company's inventory.

Necks were strained as everyone crowded around to see him check some mechanical fitting, adjust the hood slightly, tap the base with a brass hammer and finally plug it into a socket. He took a deep breath and turned it on. The whirr of the motor ignited a roar of joy from the men. Handshakes all round and a sudden outburst of *Hang Out Your Washing On The Siegfried Line.*

In the middle of the throng, Fred produced a small paintbrush and, this time, a pot of gold paint. The cowling of the motor was opened and with a great show of pomp he painted the number 1,000 and the date in gold gothic letters.

Tom, still in his overalls, nodded: "Thank you, Mr Hitler, and thank you men!" More cheers erupted as he shouted that Mr Carey was buying the drinks at the Pig & Whistle.

The men melted away into the factory and things quietened down. Tom slumped on a trolley, with his long legs stretched out in front of him. He wanted to have a word with Fred but he couldn't find him anywhere.

A clanging of metal in the middle of the assembly hall pinpointed Fred, who was now approaching Tom with another motor.

"That's enough for today, Fred. We'll start the next 1,000 on Monday."

Keeping his head stuck inside the cowling of the motor, Carey called back, "No, Mr Dartry, this is the 1,000th. I made a mistake in my calculations."

"You never make mistakes like that. What's your game?"

Fred ignored Tom long enough to place four screws into the back of the motor casing and, using a pump screwdriver, put the finishing touches to the motor. It was two minutes before six o'clock. "If you'll just hold on a minute, Mr Dartry, I'm almost finished." He cleaned the casing with a cloth and plugged in the motor. It whirred loudly. "Sounds good to me. As works manager, I declare this motor fully tested and accepted into the inventory of Albion Engineering. Now Mr Dartry, what were you saying?"

Tom persisted. "I said you don't make mistakes in your calculations."

"Right," said Fred. "I was exaggerating a little. We needed to have 1,000 motors available for despatch at the end of the week."

"But we have that already!"

Fred twitched his head slightly and winked. "You're right

again." He then picked up his paint brush and pot of silver paint. Carefully, he prised open the final motor and inscribed "1001" with the date.

"Have you gone over the edge or something. What are you up to?"

"Mr Dartry, the 1,000th motor should never be delivered to the Ministry. I think we should keep it in Albion as a trophy. I'd like you to have it in your office because we couldn't have done it without you or your chains."

"Fred, you old sod," Tom almost blushed with embarrassment. "You're right. We should keep it. I'll get Bill Henderson in Stockley to mount it on a piece of walnut. But I don't want it in my office. It belongs out here in full view of the men who built the others."

Now it was Fred's turn to look a little confused. "Why?"

"Damn it, Fred, they'll need every bit of encouragement to do the same next week!"

Chapter Notes

In the early years of the Second World War, Germany's most conspicuous advantage was the skill with which its generals employed their lead in technologically-advanced armaments, such as tanks, tactical fighter aircraft and mechanised infantry transport, to overwhelm opposition by their superior mobility. On the British side, the success of radar and its own new eight-gun fighter aircraft prevented the Luftwaffe from winning aerial control for the projected invasion of Britain and showed that, given time, British military technology might draw ahead of the enemy.

However, the economic battle had also been joined and once Hitler declared war on the US after the Japanese attack on Pearl Harbor in December 1941, it was the beginning of the end. The Western allies aided Russian war efforts by supplying trucks, aircraft and tanks which were sent in spite of grave losses at sea. By summer 1943, the Anglo-American supply lines were no longer in peril since the combination of American mass production of shipping and British technical devices for the protection of convoys was winning the battle of the Atlantic.

Reference Notes

[1]Robert Owen (1771-1858), from Lanark in Scotland, was in many respects the forerunner of modern method study. He showed an interest in the problems of layout and the need for new methods to embody better working conditions, and in making provision in the 'time allowed' for a job to cover the effects of fatigue. He reasoned that it was to his advantage, as well as to that of his employees, to improve the lot of his workers, so he introduced shorter working hours and better working conditions in his cotton spinning mill. His humanitarian concern extended to building a model village for 1,300 people.

But the real spur to work study was provided during the latter part of the nineteenth century by Frank and Lillian Gilbreth. The Gilbreths were attracted to the study of human motions and the analysis of human actions with their elementary motions. Through the analysis of these elementary motions they sought ways to improve them or eliminate them.

In 1885, Frank Gilbreth worked for a building contractor and began learning the bricklayer's trade. By the beginning of 1900 he was in the construction business on his own account and sought to analyse the skills of bricklaying. He studied the movements of his workmen during bricklaying operations and readily saw how to make improvements in their methods by substituting shorter and less fatiguing motions for more tiring existing ones.

He photographed a bricklayer at work and by studying of these photographs made further improvements in output among his men. He investigated the best scaffolding to use and invented one that could be raised a short distance at a time, so that it could carry a shelf for holding the bricks and mortar at the most convenient height for the bricklayers, thereby eliminating the need to pick up a brick from the ground. He used low-paid labourers to sort out the bricks and place them on wooden frames in such a way that the best face and end were turned in a given direction. This made it unnecessary for the bricklayer to examine the bricks so he was able to concentrate solely on bricklaying.

Mortar and bricks were positioned so that a bricklayer could pick up a brick with one hand and a trowel full of mortar with the other at the same time. Gilbreth also arranged for the mortar to be kept at such a consistency that the bricks could be pushed into place in the wall by hand. In fact, Gilbreth reduced the number of motions for laying a brick from 18 to 5, and his men, who had formerly worked to their limit to lay 1,000 bricks per day each, were able after a short period of instruction to reach a daily output of 2,700 bricks each. (The approved daily output in Britain today is only between 400 and 800 bricks.)

Interest among British industrialists in time and motion studies did not develop until the end of the First World War and it took a further 20 years before the British government gave its seal of approval to the theory. Government backing of work study techniques manifested itself in the Production Efficiency Board, which was created to run government-sponsored courses in motion studies based on Gilbreth's teaching. At the same time the Ministry of Labour sponsored a 'training within industry' scheme for supervisors.

Chapter Seven – 1939

"This is the people's war. It is our war. We are the fighters. Fight it then. Fight it with all that is in us. And may God defend the right." – Mrs Miniver

"Do you want the good news or the bad news first, Mr Dartry?"

Tom looked straight into the eyes of the officer, who returned the stare briefly, blinked and looked at the report again. Sensing he had won a small victory over the man, Tom replied, "Good, please."

"You can have your three men back from Empire. Your report is quite convincing. A 29.8 per cent jump in output in three days. We'd like to think you can sustain this, so we want you to double your capacity at Mansfield!"

"I thought I asked for the good news."

"That is the good news." Relishing Tom's obvious unease the officer continued. "And the bad news is we also want you to commence separate production in Scotland."

Tom shook his head in disbelief. "Are you daft?"

"We thought you might react like that, but, Mr Dartry, your production is too valuable. We can't afford to let anything happen to it."

"When?"

"By Christmas."

It was the middle of October.

"It's not possible," Tom said, hoping to call the officer's bluff.

"We think you can do it." The officer allowed a thin smile to form on his lips.

Tom bit his lower lip a moment, thanked the officer for getting his three men back and left. On the trip back to Mansfield, he wondered how much of the company would need to change to meet these new demands. It would be a case of new chains, extra chains and long-distance chains, something they had never contemplated before.

As the Napier turned off the main road, Tom saw Fred, smoking a cigarette and deep in thought, outside the works entrance. He got out of the car slowly and told his plant manager they had their work cut out for them in the months ahead. Fred interrupted. What about the men? Fred breathed a sigh of relief when he heard his three workers would be back in Mansfield by the end of the week. Keep the men together, Fred now urged Tom, and they'll worry about new factories and production targets later.

Over the next few days, Tom and Fred, taking refuge in Helen's kitchen, sat huddled with dozens of blueprints of the Albion works. Endless quantities of tracing paper were pinned over the drawings onto the well-scrubbed kitchen table. Circles were pencilled on different parts of the paper and heated arguments developed over where the new links in the chain should be located. At the heart of the issue was whether, in order to double production at Mansfield, they should keep their existing chain intact and develop a facsimile of it in an adjoining factory, or whether to shut down the entire plant and build a huge new custom-made factory. For the moment, any thoughts of manufacturing in Scotland were pushed to one side.

Cups of tea, stubs of pencils and cigarette ash all vied for space on the table as the two men debated the future shape of the company. Both played devil's advocate since neither knew the real answer. Tom would point out he had too much capital locked up in the existing plant to write it off and start again. He had more than enough orders to fill. Just as Fred was accepting the logic of this argument, Tom would say it was also a once-in-a-lifetime chance to build from scratch and put all they had learned about chains into a totally new plant. For a while, the argument could have gone either way.

Weary of the Mansfield stalemate, they turned to Scotland. The ministry had already built several well-camouflaged factories, which they euphemistically called 'green field' plants. In truth, they were more like grey flint sites, being located at the foot of an obscure mountain. Their only redeeming factor was they appeared to be safe from aerial attack!

When Tom had discovered that his new plant, located

between Perth and Auchterarder, was virtually inaccessible by road, it was obvious this factory was never meant to operate on economic grounds. Instead of using three-ton trucks to deliver raw materials and collect motors, he would be forced to set up a relay team of lighter vehicles ferrying goods round the clock. But in Scotland, at least, it would be possible to start the chains from scratch. They could experiment quickly with new ideas and feed them back to Mansfield. The only real problem would be labour. Tom had been incensed at the ministry's suggestion that he use local youths for the production line. When he told them it took years to train an engineer and many months for an assembly line worker, they simply suggested he should innovate.

With their thoughts firmly fixed in the distant Highlands, neither Tom nor Fred noticed the sound of the low-flying aircraft until it was almost over them. In hot pursuit was a second fighter, with all guns blazing. The two men threw themselves onto the floor and Tom shouted to Helen to stay with their two children. Large-calibre machine gun fire raked the cottage, ripping through walls, shattering windows and splintering woodwork.

Outside the cottage, the same fusillade had stitched a pattern in the road and continued across to the Albion factory. Smoke was now pouring out of shattered skylights and men were running, shouting, and carrying buckets of water.

Half an hour later, Tom, smelling of smoke and looking like a chimney sweep, stood in his vegetable garden with Helen, his three-and-a-half year old son James and ten-month-old George, all of whom had miraculously escaped injury in the attack. Peering into her wrecked kitchen, Helen screamed: "The Ascot is ruined!"

Intentional or not, the strafing of the cottage and factory had forced Tom to make a decision about the future of the Mansfield plant. He would not risk having his entire production wiped out by a raid. It would have to be two Mansfield factories, two separate chains, and hope that at least one would survive.

Work began at once on the new factory, which was called the North Works for it lay due north of the existing factory. Architectural drawings were prepared and provisional floor layouts were drawn up. Copies of these were pinned to a notice board in the South Works so Albion's workers could see the shape of things to come.

Fred by now had been sent to examine the new Scottish plant and to oversee the installation of equipment. Once operational, he was to take as many Mansfield men as he needed to get production running and to start training local labour.

On one of Fred's few days in Mansfield, the consulting engineer on the new North Works project stormed into a makeshift office at the edge of the site. Fred sat him down, still fuming, and poured him a cup of tea with a dash of whisky. The new plant's foundry had suddenly become the centre of an emotional issue as the Albion workers defiantly maintained that the blueprints were unworkable. There were better ways to lay out the machinery, they said. Gathering up the blueprints, Fred strode over to the partially finished building.

"Right! My little mutineers," he barked at about a dozen men. "Who's minding the store?" The men shuffled uneasily at the sight of Carey.

"So you think you can lay out the plant better," Fred snapped at them. Sounding like a sergeant major with a platoon of new recruits he shouted that he wanted a workable plan by the end of the day, and didn't give a damn what it looked like. Fred ordered the building contractor's crew to stop work and then barricaded himself in his shed with the consulting engineer and a half dozen substantial sandwiches bursting with corned beef for the rest of the day.

Suddenly realising they had won more control over their new factory design than they had expected, the mutinous dozen set to work with perhaps only a slight trace of panic. Large empty crates were moved around to simulate the position of various functions, men paced off distances, shook their heads and moved the crates again and again. Countless floor configurations were tried and discarded until they found a layout that appeared to work.

The pair of half-built furnaces, of course, had to remain in place, but the core and pattern shops, instead of being placed to the left of the furnaces, were now located on either side of them and the all-important fettling shop, which had been located at the far end of the foundry, was now moved closer to the centre. Short conveyor belts could be installed linking this final phase of the foundry with subsequent milling, turning and heat treatment areas before heading into the general machine shop. Cabling was re-routed, door frames repositioned, spaces for new windows were chalked on the recently built walls.

Holes were knocked in the walls to give more ventilation in what would be a sweltering foundry. Some of these holes were stuffed with bottles with their bottoms cut off and facing neck first into the foundry. If extra ventilation was needed, corks in the necks of the bottles would be removed, allowing streams of fresh air to circulate the foundry.

Not all the changes were necessary, but having embarked on the upheaval, the 12 mutineers now felt obliged to leave as little of the engineer's blueprints intact as possible.

As promised, or threatened, Fred returned to the new foundry at the end of the day. It had changed beyond recognition. Proudly the men lined up in two orderly ranks in front of their work area. Eyeing the mock military inspection from a distance, Tom walked over to investigate. He saw Fred and the engineer milling around the men and inspecting what had been done to the core of the new factory. Fred seemed pleased, the engineer less so.

Tom arrived at the comic scene just as the engineer bade goodbye to Fred. The engineer, pausing for a moment, turned to Tom and said: "Never, Mr Dartry, never let your workers design their workplace." With this well-intentioned advice, the engineer disappeared into the distance. Taking a closer look at the ground plan the men had concocted, Tom confided to Fred that they might have lost a consultant engineer, but they had gained a more efficient way to make castings.

Tom's remaining problem was finding enough men, or more likely women, to fill the places on the assembly line in both Mansfield and Scotland. Once more he felt like a military commander, trying to judge the correct disposition of his resources, of where and when to place his key troops. Some of his more experienced hands were dispersed into different shifts throughout the Mansfield and Scottish factories in the hope that some form of order and discipline would be maintained.

Trying to get young and inexperienced new workers – some of whom had never seen the inside of a factory – into a routine proved to be a major stumbling block. It didn't take long for Tom, Fred and every shift foreman to know that the training should have been done over a period of months, rather than trying to get raw recruits into the factory from the outset. But they were stuck with the mess and had to see their way out of it. Production suffered.

Now with the new Mansfield plant coming into operation, Tom realised he didn't have enough men with the right skills to run the factory efficiently. As he feared, output of the two plants barely matched the volume achieved by the single old factory. Some portions of the North Works, which was officially opened in January 1940, operated like precision clockwork and quickly built up large inventories of components, while others suddenly emerged as bottlenecks. It was difficult to get the foundry to produce the right castings at the right time. On one day Tom had to order the melting down of a batch of half-horsepower bodies because there were already 500 castings in store and no scrap or pig iron to make the quarter-horsepower bodies that were urgently needed.

Things improved slightly when a Ministry official suggested they use a stock allocation method. Having used the 'maximum-minimum' approach for years, Fred was hesitant to try anything so radical as a new way of planning production.[1] In the new approach, castings were ordered in small quantities on account of the wide range of products made. But the order would include one or two more than the number actually needed, thereby building up a sufficient stock of castings to meet unexpected jobs. When the number of castings in stock rose beyond a certain level, subsequent orders for new castings would be reduced.

With the new North Works gearing up for full production, attention quickly focused on the couple of acres of land separating the two factories. Dig for Victory was the official call to the British people – feed yourself and win the war! To this end, the Albion workers enthusiastically surveyed unused parts of the Mansfield site and every keen gardener was soon locked in battle over what were the ideal crops to plant.

Tom tried to stay aloof from the vegetable debate, noting

wryly that it took a day to get a new foundry plan out of the men but it was taking weeks to decide what should be grown on a couple of open fields. However, when he heard that potatoes, followed by leeks, were likely to win the day over sprouts – his favourite vegetable – he urged a compromise planting of all three. He would even donate some space at the back of his cottage to produce vegetables for the communal pot in the works canteen, where anyone could now get 'meat and two veg with sweet to follow' for ninepence.

Helen resisted this magnanimous gesture – it was mid-1940 and she was now pregnant with their third child – and scolded Tom for his generosity and short-sightedness. They needed the vegetables for themselves, she said. Anyway, if they did grow a lot of extra vegetables, they could always do what James Fairfax had done. Barter them, maybe for some nice strawberries in June. Tom, finding his mouth beginning to water, called a halt to the conversation. They would give the works canteen whatever land they could afford this year, and hopefully things would be better in 1941.

Against this background was set the episode of the lemon. One of Albion's first volunteers, by now fighting somewhere in North Africa, somehow managed to send a present of a lemon to his wife. An exotic luxury in peacetime, but even more so during these troubled times. But not knowing what to do with the small piece of fruit, she gave it to Fred who decided to raffle it. Hundreds of cloakroom tickets were sold at a brisk pace and the proceeds – in excess of £17 – were donated to the Women's Voluntary Service for children who had moved up to Mansfield from London at the outbreak of the war.

A loud cheer erupted as a fitter from the works maintenance shop with the winning ticket collected the lemon from Fred. The lucky fitter ceremoniously brought it home where it was admired by family and friends alike for several days. But then he too decided he didn't really want it and donated to the local church Grand Spring raffle, where it was duly won by someone in a nearby village. It was rumoured that the lemon, beginning to show its age by now, was spotted at another raffle later in the year.

Fruit and vegetables aside, Tom remained preoccupied

with the problem of skilled labour. Finally, he decided to take the tongue-in-cheek advice of the Ministry to heart. He would innovate.

Tom devised a two-pronged attack on his labour problem. The first entailed an unusual recruiting drive. He contacted Rev. Colliston, Mansfield's local vicar, who with the help of the committee of the Women's Institute drew up a list of pensioners who had either engineering or factory experience. Many were veterans from the Great War and a few had even seen action in the Boer War. Afflicted with rheumatism, arthritis, poor eyesight and bad hearing, they were hardly the model of an efficient workforce. But as a whole they had done every kind of job imaginable – there were joiners, saddlers, coopers and tailors. They were all that Tom could find and they would do for now.

Tom had several wooden sheds from the Albion site dismantled and the timbers used to patch and repair the church hall, which would house the new brigade of workers. Albion thus found itself with a third factory in Mansfield. Soon the little church hall was humming, literally, with activity; old tunes from the previous wars were echoing through the building. Husbands and wives frequently worked in pairs, relieving the tedium and making cups of tea.

The pensioners could not be paid on a piece-work basis as their output was much less than many of their juniors in the main factory, although their quality was often superior. Instead, Tom decided to pay the war workers an efficiency bonus which had recently been introduced in America. In this, if a team worked 200 hours in a week and completed a number of jobs whose schedule time was 220 hours, the average efficiency would be 110 per cent. The schedule times were based on the factory standard times. If efficiency fell below 50 per cent then a weekly wage was paid. Tom devised an efficiency scale on which up to a maximum 33 per cent bonus was paid for 150 efficiency.

Elizabeth Colliston, the vicar's daughter, was responsible for the hall and the workforce of 18 veterans. She kept morale high among her workers by dividing them into smaller groups and pitting them against each other. Intuitively, she banned the eating of any sweets with wrappers, knowing full well how difficult and time consuming it would be for her elderly workforce to cope with removing the wrappers.

Despite the regular consumption of bags of bon-bons and glucose sweets by the pensioners, Elizabeth noticed that output slowed each afternoon at about 4 o'clock. In the hope of reversing this drop-off in production, she conducted a little experiment by borrowing her father's gramophone and set it up in the hall. By 3.45 she had also prepared 18 mugs of tea which she dispensed to the upbeat rhythms of Vivaldi's *Four Seasons* and Bizet's *Carmen*. The sound emanating from the Church hall was more reminiscent of afternoon tea at the Ritz than a small factory producing motor components.

Undoubtedly, these pensioners were a help, but Tom knew the bulk of the work would still need to be done by fully trained and able men. And as the Government conscripted a further 250,000 men to reinforce the British Expeditionary Force now operating in France, his chances of finding new men, and even holding onto his existing workforce, were dwindling rapidly. He then embarked on the second part of his battle for labour – a new labour chain would have to be built, this one spanning the Atlantic.

From his own experience in the Great War, Tom was keenly aware that long, tenuous supply chains can lose battles. But he couldn't wait for the US to join Britain and her allies in the fight against Hitler. It was March 1940 and Tom Dartry needed men now! If Tom managed to recruit enough engineering and design staff from America, it would give him a head start if and when the US joined the conflict.

The US embassy in London supplied countless lists of East Coast engineering companies and Tom finally stumbled across Tri-State Manufacturing and Engineering Inc. of Albany, New York. Tri-State, substantially bigger than Albion, appeared to employ a similar range of engineering skills yet the two companies manufactured very different products. Tom now offered the American company an option on the distribution of Albion's engineering output, on condition they supplied Albion with the necessary manpower for the duration of the war. This presupposed that Albion would survive.

Tom undertook the hazardous trip to New York in late March to meet the board of Tri-State. Generous distribution terms were offered and the Tri-State board agreed to ask for volunteers. Tom Dartry insisted that he be allowed to put his case to the men personally.

It wasn't the best of times, nor was it the worst of times in Europe. The real fighting had not begun and there was hope that the German armies would remain where they were. For the moment, France, Denmark, Holland and Belgium were safe and Britain had almost 200,000 men bolstering the French defences. If Tom had made his appeal three months later following the rapid collapse of every army on the continent and the humiliating evacuation of the British Expeditionary Force at Dunkirk, things may not have gone his way.

For the moment, however, he argued that if America declared war on Germany, most of the eligible men gathered in front of him would be conscripted and sent to fight. His new safe Scottish factory needed skilled men and once they were in Britain, they were unlikely to be called into action. The offer was open only to single men. They would be paid American rates for American output levels. They would be given special food and clothing allowances and, finally, their jobs in Tri-State would be open for them on their return. He then moved onto a more emotional level. Tom knew full well these men, the backbone of American industrial might, were intensely patriotic and he needed to tap into this. He warned them that if Britain fell, America would be isolated in the world. All her allies would have been vanquished and America would be in peril. This was a battle against barbarism and a fight for freedom itself.

To the board's surprise and Tom's relief, the plea produced three volunteers – all with distant English backgrounds and all eager to support England in her darkest hour. Within a couple of days, Tom had secured transport for his new Albion recruits and after innumerable farewell drinks with those left behind, they departed.

It rained remorselessly on their arrival in Croydon, South London, and the three American tradesmen joked non-stop about rain and fog not being mentioned in their contracts. But once they piled into the back of the Bedford three-tonner and started the journey through London and on to the Mansfield factory in the Midlands, the humour evaporated. Countless shops had boarded their windows against bomb damage while sandbag barricades protected important civic buildings. There were signs everywhere of a nation bracing itself for an onslaught. But they brightened up again as the truck made its way through the edge of the Sherwood Forest and eventually arrived on the outskirts of Mansfield.

Tom had planned production in the Scottish factory on a two-shift basis. Now with the new recruits going through two weeks of training in Mansfield before moving to Scotland, and the prospect of more to follow, he began to consider a full three-shift schedule. Skilled labour, even if it had to be imported three thousand miles, would no longer hold back production. Over the next year, Tom steadily augmented his American workforce until they numbered 25. When concentrated at the Scottish plant, this was sufficient for the Americans to put their stamp on the works and the way it operated.

No sooner had he begun to solve his manpower problems, than the first real heavy fighting of the war began. The Battle of Britain was swiftly followed by the Blitz in September 1940. Tom boarded up the Queen Street office and hoped it would survive. The company's warehouses in south London took several direct hits and were effectively destroyed. Everything was now concentrated in Mansfield and Scotland.

As the air war intensified, Albion was inundated with requests for more basic machined parts, which meant expanded use of Mansfield's foundries. The company was soon making anti-aircraft gun components, searchlight assemblies, shell casings, gun carriages, aircraft propellers, and mobile laundry machines.

The rate of obsolescence, about which the various ministries had warned Albion, had been greater than anyone had foreseen. New designs, new materials, new products, even new machines to make them with. They all came crowding in at the same time. To meet this unexpected demand for new products, Tom was forced to set up an enlarged design department since many of the engineering drawings he received from ministry draftsmen or third-party contractors were inaccurate or potentially misleading.

A Macready-inspired review of every new piece of equipment, and its drawings, was initiated. With two young draftsmen in tow, Macready poured over each set of plans, calling out rhetorical questions – is this supposed to be water-proof? Will this be transported by air or on a truck? Will it survive a 500ft drop by parachute? After dissecting the blue-prints, Macready's team produced their own drawings which were then passed on to Fred.[2]

Fred soon discovered that the pace of design was acceler-ating too quickly for both the engineering and assembly workers so he requested a meeting with Macready and Tom. It was impossible, he complained, to make 10 new different things if the factory was geared up to make only one or two. He needed to know what the priorities were and he would be able to mass produce them. Macready could stick to the one-offs.

Macready grunted in agreement.

Production on the factory floor, Fred argued, could only make tried and tested products. Macready could experiment with a small assembly line if he wanted, and the real matter of making products should be left to Fred. A small portion of the men could be allocated to experimental work and testing – this he recognised was necessary – but once that was completed, the work would enter a production phase. None the less, because of Tom's chains, he argued that his men had to be capable of working both on existing products and new developments. And some compromise, he suggested, would be needed over the Time Study measurements[3] used to assess pay rates. Fred and most of his men firmly believed in the 'fair day's pay for a fair day's work' school of thought and any 'slackers' or 'shirkers' in the company were ruthlessly weeded out by the men themselves.

Finally, if they were to get the best out of the men, they had to get out and see more. Fred wanted his men to see tests and field trials, even target practice. But most of all, he wanted to see German motors and castings, because the men needed to know if their production was better than the enemy's.

And so it went on. As the *Bismarck* was hunted and sunk in one of the greatest sea chases in maritime history, production of Albion's bread and butter items – electric motors – grew and eventually passed the 1,500 threshold. Like a well-oiled machine, this part of the company was the most productive.

By now, Fred was also able to boost production at the Scottish plant by giving the independent-minded Americans considerably more latitude in their running of the factory than existed at Mansfield. Seven-day production was halted only briefly – not by the much feared German air raids but by a small avalanche which swept away several light vehicles and some of the stores, fortunately without casualties.

Although well past his normal retirement age, Macready was everywhere. On regular unofficial visits to the likes of Hawkers and Vickers, he checked for basic flaws in some of their mechanical designs and scoured for opportunities for Albion to introduce its own products. Invariably clutching an old brown briefcase stuffed full of confidential blueprints, Macready was a regular sight in the design 'lofts' of these aircraft manufacturers and became one of the best walking advertisements that Albion could have hoped for.

Whenever Macready, Tom and the rest of the Albion plant thought they had succeeded in one area, new demands would surface in another. Output had to be raised. Standards had to be consistently high. New designs had to be implemented. And operating profits had to be scrupulously checked to insure that ministry work was being fairly charged. Profiteering, an ugly spectre from the First World War, had already tarnished some reputations in the industry.

For the next three years, a relentless pace of activity produced countless thousands of motors, windings, aircraft sub-assemblies, gun barrels and even torpedoes and shell casings. Everything that Albion could produce was thrown into the war effort. Every last inch of factory space and surrounding land was employed in an all-out effort to defeat the enemy.

Towards the end of 1944, after the Allied landings in Normandy and the start of the V2 rocket campaign against Britain, Tom had an unexpected visit from the directors at Tri-State, the New York company that was continuing to supply him with men for the Scottish factory. Tri-State's own production was expanding and they were looking to see what type of product they could expect from Albion now that the war was almost over.

A haggard, balding Tom Dartry, showing every one of his

55 years, stared back at the directors with a blank expression. "Well, you can imagine, we've been busy with a lot of other things recently," Tom tried to joke with the dour Tri-State directors, but he saw it had no effect. "We have a few designs that could be adapted to peace time. Or we could let you have a marvellous little washer and drier combination, but it might need a bit of updating."

A small angular man stepped forward. "Mr Dartry, we had hoped for something designed in this decade," he quietly scowled. "Why don't we have a chat with this Macready guy? He can show us what he's working on and maybe we can use some of the ideas back Stateside."

With an overwhelming sense of resignation, Tom agreed, knowing that Albion risked giving away so much of its hard-earned research and development. Tom felt a touch of anger, not with the Americans, who had only come to collect their part of the bargain. But with himself, for he now realised he had really lost the ability to fight. He and the rest of Albion would make certain that Germany would be finished off. But after that, he wasn't too sure. In some ways, he felt like an exhausted heavyweight boxer. Asked first to fight 10 rounds, he then discovers that another five pulverising rounds are necessary to beat his opponent. And just at the end of Round 15, he's told to go back into the ring for five more rounds. Tom felt it was Round 20, and he couldn't take much more. In his heart, he knew he had failed to plan for one thing. Peace!

But there was also a deep personal reason for his change of mood. During the course of the previous decade, he had spent virtually every waking moment thinking about Albion. And he had watched from a distance as his young family – James, George and Elinor – began to grow up without really knowing him. It was something he had not bargained for and now was the time to do something about it! As soon as peace was declared, he would retire!

Chapter Notes

Profound changes were soon under way in peace-time Britain. Much of the industrial infrastructure of the country had been destroyed during the course of the war and efforts to rebuild it were hampered by shortages of critical equipment, raw materials and labour. Adding further pressure to an already stretched economy was the severe winter of 1946/47 which forced large sections of British industry to shut down for lack of fuel.

Fortunately, the severity of this weather highlighted the dangerous state into which Britain and other European countries had fallen and gave fresh impetus to American plans to underwrite the reconstruction of the shattered western European economies.

Agreed during the summer of 1947, the massive Marshall Aid programme, named after US Secretary of State George Marshall, effectively rescued Europe from collapse. Britain, which received a quarter of the total Marshall Aid funds, would prove to be the largest beneficiary of the programme. But before this Marshall Aid arrived, many companies found it well nigh impossible to conduct business on a normal basis. One feature article in *The Financial Times* (May 12, 1947), headlined "Morris Motors from the Inside", captured the mood of the times and graphically illustrated the precarious state of affairs facing British industry in the immediate post-war years (see Appendix).

Reference Notes

[1]Fred Carey was understandably reluctant to tinker with something as fundamental as a stock allocation method in the plant. In reality, a standard allocation method worked in quite a simple fashion and was easily understood by everyone in the factory. For example, when the stock clerk received a list of the castings required for a specific job he went through the records, entering in pencil under the appropriate headings the job number and quantity reserved, and adjusted the stock figure under the heading of 'available'. The available stock was the number of castings available after all known orders had been satisfied, while the active stock was the number of castings actually in stock, although many of these might be reserved for specific job orders.

The stock clerk concerned himself with the available stock and not with the actual stock. If the available stock was not high enough to meet demand, he placed a requisition with the foundry for further supplies. When these castings were received both the available and actual stock figures were increased.

Despite the crucial importance of the work, stock clerks and storemen were never regarded as having high status within any factory. A contemporary narrative (*Engineering Factory Supplies* by W. J. Hislox, Pitman, 1926) recounts: "In the large works the store-keeper enjoys a fairly high status, but not as high as he should do, considering his responsibilities. It is not everyone's ambition to become a storekeeper, and the post is rarely offered to the young fellows in the works who will ultimately occupy high executive positions. The position of storekeeper is distinctly middle-class, and makes no appeal to industrial aristocrats.

"As one man expressed it, 'Those college chaps are "bagging" most of the positions, but they are leaving the store severely alone.' In smaller works, the position is much worse. It is a good job for the type of man who regards a salary of £3 to £4 a week as the utmost he can expect to earn."

[2]Macready's design philosophy by this stage boiled down to the modern equivalent of 'getting it right first time.' Despite his best efforts to find out how effective his designs were in the field, crucial feedback on even elementary design features was difficult to obtain. But when field reports suggested that design changes should take place, this triggered an avalanche of additional, and by rights quite unnecessary, engineering work that played havoc with efficient production within the Albion plant.

For instance, a simple component like a bracket which could be drawn, or redrawn, in a few minutes could take days to prepare for manufacture. A standard procedure was that every part had to have its drawings approved for manufacture first by the works manage-ment and planning engineer, together with the appropriate produc-tion engineer. They set out a layout which showed how it was proposed to machine the part. The layout gave the details of the jigs, tools and gauges which would be necessary for each operation and the most suitable machine tool. The jigs, tools and gauges were then made and once the initial batch was machined, a time study assess-ment was applied to get standard times for piece work. All this detail would be recorded in a master route card, a copy of which was placed in a fireproof safe so that production could be re-started in case of damage to the works.

[3]In the eyes of the Albion workforce, time study – the most common and important means of measuring repetitive work – was a neces-sary evil. Originated in the US by Frederick Winslow Taylor (1856-

1915), time study called for the job under investigation to be broken down into a number of elements. The cycle time for each element is then measured a number of times. This gives a set of observed times for all the elements of the job. It is at this point that difficulties arise because the analyst must use his own judgment to assess the rate of working for each element. In addition to this rating he must also judge the operator he is observing against a hypothetical normal or standard operator. It is then possible to estimate a basic time where

$$\text{Basic time} = \frac{\text{Observed times average} \times \text{Observed rating}}{\text{Standard rating}}$$

Basic time, however, takes no account of necessary pauses for rest and personal needs. Once this is applied a Standard time emerges which is the basis for most payment systems. The difference between Basic time and Standard time is commonly 33 per cent.

Another approach to work measurement is Synthesis, in which the time for a job is built up from the total of element times previously defined or from time studies on other jobs.

Finally, times may be calculated using Predetermined Motion Time Systems (PMTS) whereby times established for basic elements are built up to give the time for a job at a defined level of performance. The PMT system was first used in the US in 1924 when Motion Time Analysis was introduced. The other principal systems are Work Factor System (US), Method Time Measurement (USSR) and Basic Motions Study (Canada).

In addition to his work on time study, F.W. Taylor was also responsible for laying the foundations of the general science of management and the recognition of management as a profession. During the 1884-86 period, Taylor was manager of the machine shop of the Midvale Steel Company, which cast and machined heavy forgings. He found that men were inefficient from lack of understanding their craft and that much time was wasted due to poor planning of work.

Taylor declared that much of the blame lay with management, who should promote co-operation rather than antagonism. The first essential was scientific rate-fixing based on time study of the operations themselves. Before a time study could be made the management had to collect, analyse and codify existing craft knowledge. Taylor was a remarkable man, who used uncommon tact and great resolution to get his theory into practice. Output, as a result of his ideas, often doubled or trebled and the men were less fatigued. He paid extraordinarily high wages, often 50 to 100 per cent higher than before, in spite of which costs per piece were lower.

After leaving Midvale, Taylor acted as a consultant in the reorganisation of a number of works, including the very large Bethlehem steelworks, which he studied in 1898. It was here that he carried out his famous experiments on shovelling coal. He reduced the number of shovellers from 600 to 140 and, by substituting broad shovels for the narrow spades formerly used, orchestrated a gigantic leap in productivity. Despite wages being increased by 60 per cent for the shovellers, Bethlehem managed to save a staggering $78,000 a year as a direct result of Taylor's analysis.

Chapter Eight – 1959

Buddy Holly dies; trials of the first Hovercraft; BMC launches the Mini; opening of the M1; Hawker Siddeley and de Havilland merge

"I hate their speeches," Fred gritted his teeth, "specially at things like this, but let me tell you a few things about Albion."

Fred Carey stood at the bar of the Central Hotel in Manchester and, catching the eye of a barman, ordered another round of drinks for his young engineering apprentices. In 15 minutes, they were due to accept their training awards and Fred knew they'd need to steady their nerves. He too was due on stage shortly to collect his own 30-year service citation and watch.

"Don't listen to what they say about Tom Dartry. The war didn't break him – he still had lots of fight left. I remember how he saw the Yanks off good and proper. Tri-State came over to collect their pound of flesh. It was a bit like that old story of making a pact with the devil, Prometheus or someone, you have to pay up some day. They saw heaps of potential in Macready's ideas. The old boy had been beavering away on hydraulic systems for aircraft and was coming up with some very clever ideas.

"The Yanks, God bless them, did the picking and choosing. Tom let them do that. They were about to start manufacturing some of our neat ideas, as they called them, when Tom pointed out they could only sell equipment actually manufactured by Albion. They hadn't read their contracts very closely. They got very shirty about it and began calling us ungrateful for winning the war. Some pretty blunt stuff. Tom was an officer and could handle this sort of mess. He started quoting the Merchant of Venice, the quality of mercy is not something or other. Then he simply said, Gentlemen, let's negotiate.

"I was there for that, a real moment to savour. We weren't wriggling out of anything, just stopping the house being ransacked by our cousins. I think they respected us more for it. We both got good deals and Tri-State manufactured some of the hydraulics under licence in the US.

"We didn't need trouble like this at the time. We were trying to change our whole production, switch over to new products and integrate a lot of new faces. We had to let most of the women go once the men returned from Germany and France. To give Tom his due, he kept on the girls. I think Macready was behind that as well.

"No sooner had we got some of the production sorted out, we were hit by the weather. I have never seen anything like that winter. Everything covered in snow, and more snow. The winter of 46/47 was a nightmare. Plant had to close everywhere, we weren't the only ones. At least, Empire was having a tough time too.

"Coal was in short supply and what was left couldn't be moved because the roads were blocked. Factories just shut down. This was real hardship. We sent people home, and told them to come back when the weather improved.

"Bill Ferguson, he worked in the machine shop, a doughty fellow if there ever was one. Bill had a young family, everyone seemed to have young families then, and Bill felt he had to be in work to be paid. He trudged through the snow with a bicycle. When the snow worsened, he tied the bicycle to his back and went cross country. How he did it, I'll never know. As he pushed the bike through the front gates, he was whistling as if nothing was amiss. I gave him some tea, thanked him for coming, told him he'd be paid anyway and sent him home again. When the others heard this the following week, they felt it reflected badly on them. What was he doing, said one, f***ing flying?"

Fred and the apprentices laughed.

"Once things returned to normal, and Tom had seen off the Americans, I thought he'd settle back into his job. I was wrong; he's a determined git when he wants to be, and it cuts both ways. To his credit, he did everything for Albion.

"He went up to London to see some of Jimmy Fairfax's old cronies at the Delphinium. Tom always believed management had to be good, and now wanted someone to take us over. He still had a key stake in the company and wanted to be a silent partner if they brought some new management blood into

Albion. He had three young children by this stage, so he wanted to safeguard their future too.

"I remember him coming back to the plant that evening, somewhat the worse for drink, shouting at the top of his voice that the whole bloody night shift was to give him a hand. We all trudged out, grinning like a bunch of idiots and there we saw his beloved old Napier, hanging over the verge of the river bank. So we all had a good laugh hauling it back onto terra firma.

"The deal was cooked up in the Club and sure enough some City bankers arrived to look at the place. Notes were made of everything. Even the cottage. Helen gave them short shrift – threw them out really – and told them that the cottage was not part of the factory. Goodbye!

"Tom quit in April '49. That was the end of the rat race for him. We gave him a gold watch, but he turned around and gave me and a few others these new Biro pens. Fifty-five shillings each, mind. A week's wage for some. It was a handsome gesture by a true gentleman.

"It's funny, you see a job being done by one man, suddenly it needs five men to do it. Once he was gone, marketing was divided into domestic and overseas, while production was split into what they called defence and household. There were freshly-scrubbed faces everywhere.

"After Tom left and all these youngsters came in – I doubt if some of them had begun to shave – the place didn't feel like a family-run thing. I lost contact with many of the men and only heard what was happening through the grapevine. There was an explosion of activity, with things happening everywhere.

"We were told to export or die. It made sense when the pound was devalued, our products were 30 per cent cheaper overseas. We started into Europe, the East, all over the place. I was even invited on a trip to Yugoslavia, I don't really know why. By then, we'd done a lot of work on the new Brabazon airliner and were getting a lot of attention because of it.

"But back in Mansfield, we discovered we needed two sets of reps, one for military and one for household. You couldn't really expect someone to know about hydraulic systems on transport planes and know their way around laundry machines at the same time. Obviously the big money was in aircraft and the like, so they got the best reps, good expenses and plenty of back-up.

"One of our best household reps on the continent turned out to be Joe Anderson. We couldn't give him much back-up. In fact, we sent him out on a one-way ticket on the logic that he'd have to sell something, anything, if he was going to make it back. He didn't speak any foreign languages, but he seemed happy once he had a catalogue and a price list. It all went quiet for a couple of months and the next thing we knew he was sending orders through on stationery from really posh hotels and asking for commission payments to be directed to The Normandy in Deauville or the Grande Hotel in Baden-Baden or wherever.

"We phoned countless times, but couldn't find him. It took us a while to figure out what was going on. Joe, in fact, wasn't much of salesman, but he was lucky. So lucky, he was spending most of his time in the casinos. He was raking in more than he could ever earn in commission. So he hired some locals to sell washers, and cookers and driers; they'd pass the orders on to him and share the commission. Joe was cleverer than we had ever imagined.

"When we heard about the gambling some of the new blood in the company took exception to it. A real puritanical streak running through them. They wanted him recalled, or sacked, or preferably both. Then Joe hit the jackpot.

"He won and lost so much money that his hosts – these Riviera hotels and gaming clubs – began to treat him as a fixture around the place, good for business you know. Big stakes, winning big and losing big. Well they couldn't obviously pay him to play, that's against any sort of rule, but they did the next best thing. They began buying Albion's kitchen machines. He told us to build the equipment with bigger capacities – real industrial or commercial scale – and right enough he started getting some good orders. He opened up a whole new market for us.

"Here at home, demand was impossible to meet, we could sell anything we could make. Having a marketing team really was the equivalent to having a third nostril, and it wasn't the best atmosphere in which to train salesmen. Empire was steaming ahead too, trying to catch us in some areas, racing ahead of us in others.

"We were never really a sales-based company. We didn't have that type of background, probably because we got kicked in the teeth in the Depression and then the war transformed us completely. During the last ten years we just churned out the stuff and it sold. Albion had a really good name, because we had such a strong engineering tradition. We could make anything mechanical, even electro-mechanical. One of our strengths was production control and planning. We had a ingenious system with Roneoed[1] shop orders and Hollerith cards.[2]

"We didn't have much of a name in continental Europe, not at first, but in the Commonwealth, something with an Albion label on it was highly prized.

"In France and Germany we were winning against the locals because we produced something that did the job and we provided the right level of service. We didn't need to compete on price. The locals could do that if they wanted. This changed after a while, though. Marketing men will tell you no market is static. We got in at a very profitable level and it took the locals a long time to catch up.

"In Australia and New Zealand, though, we were a bit too complacent. We thought we had the market by right. Sure enough, we found ourselves competing against some of the same French and German companies we were fighting just a couple of hundred miles away. Funny thing was, they were beating us in our distant markets, but we were beating them in the markets closer to home. We never really figured that one out. Maybe our lines of communication weren't all that good. They were fine as far as the Riviera and the casino towns of Europe, but not to Sydney or Auckland.

"Things were happening everywhere in Britain. We were very busy working on the new Vulcan bombers and then the Comets.[3] Empire seemed to be picking up a good bit of business too and was beginning to poach some of our engineers. It was around this time Sam Macready died. He'd done it all, and for someone in his seventies he'd lived a full life. We all bitterly missed him and I'll tell you a year hasn't gone by when we haven't needed him.

"In the middle of all this, Tom was given a knighthood. Well you could have knocked him, and us, over with a feather. He accepted it a bit reluctantly, mind. He told me it was really recognition of what the factory, all the men and the women, had achieved during the war and now with our exports. No one, apart from the board, called him Sir Thomas. There were a few old hands who still called him Mr Tom, but for most of the plant it was simply Mr Dartry. We figured the board was somehow behind the knighthood.

"Then we had a run of bad luck with the Comets, and Boeing rolled out the 707. That really beat the pants off us on range and capacity. But it also showed what you can do when there's government backing. We learnt something from the Yanks about complex one-off projects.

"Military business was still essential for us. Then there was Suez and the board thought we had too many eggs in our military basket. So blow me down, we start buying companies left, right and centre. First a radio manufacturer, then a furniture company in High Wycombe and we apparently thought of buying Daimler, but bought a small chain of cinemas instead.

"But lads, let me tell you. I respect tradition and I think Albion's traditions are worthwhile. You know, like sickness benefits, or pensions, or training. Other companies have their own ways of conducting business, not necessarily better, just different. Well, we buy a company with 200 workers and suddenly everything, the bills of material,[4] the part numbers, even the notepaper, is turned upside down, because they have to adapt to our ways. If you don't fit in, you're sacked. It gave takeovers a bad name and for the first time we started having labour troubles, you know, walk-outs and the like.

"Well, if you ask me I think our pinstripe board has strayed from the track. Power has gone to their heads. I just wonder how long Tom Dartry can sit back and watch this happen."

With that last remark, Fred gulped down his pint and called his trainees to attention. "Right," he said, "let's get our awards!"

Chapter Notes

The 1950s was a period marked by major changes in world affairs in which the post-war supremacy of the US and the Soviet Union was confirmed. It was a decade that witnessed the first United Nations-sponsored war in Korea, which also provided the shattered Japanese economy with a crucial kick-start on the road to industrial supremacy.

This period also saw the disintegration of Western Europe's colonial empires, first with the French collapse in Indo-China and later in Africa. In fact by 1956, the Anglo-French debacle at Suez demonstrated that the former imperial powers could no longer protect their far-flung interests.

Despite these overseas traumas, European countries were experiencing a political renaissance that would have profound implications for decades to come. After emerging from their acute post-war difficulties, six European nations established the European Coal and Steel Community in 1952. In less than 10 years, steel output in these member states would double without any increase in labour. It was the first step towards the creation of the Common Market, which came into existence in January 1958.

In Britain, in spite of the humiliation of Suez and troubled industrial output, Harold Macmillan was able to tell the nation by July 1957 that it "never had it so good" and that it could now put the days of shortages and rationing behind it.

Reference Notes

[1]Albion's rapidly expanding product lines during the 1950s meant that there was a corresponding increase in engineering documentation. In fact, all production control systems require the preparation and issuing of large quantities of 'paperwork'. Only with the introduction of Roneo masters was the handwriting task of the stores clerk reduced. Some works had a Master Routing Card from which different records could be prepared by using a duplicating copy. From one master card it was possible to produce a material requisition (necessary to draw material for the shop order), Hollerith Cards (a number for each operation for the time keeper to issue to the operator), the shop order itself (as agreed with the machine loading section), a progress copy (to keep production control up to date) and

finally a number of jig, tool and gauge requisitions both to warn the toolroom and withdraw those tools necessary once the job was underway.

[2]In the 1880s, Herman Hollerith developed the modern machine-readable punched card and the associated mechanical card processing equipment. Hired by the Bureau of the Census, he developed and used his inventions on the huge volume of data collected in the 1890 US census.

The presence, or absence of holes, in particular positions on a card represented the presence or absence of particular characteristics about the individual in the census. In order to read the cards, rods were passed through them. The rods made contact with a bowl of mercury to form an electrical contact and caused a counter to advance by one. The Hollerith tabulator was, therefore, the first computing machine which employed a non-mechanical processing means. It proved to be so successful that a company was set up to develop the invention. This company eventually became known as International Business Machines.

[3]Post-war British aerospace engineering took an early lead over its main competitors with the introduction of the Comet, the world's first passenger jet aircraft. This technical advantage was virtually wiped out, however, when the Comet suffered a series of crashes in the mid-1950s and the US developed the more successful rival Boeing 707. Significantly, the 707 was funded by the US Air Force which sought military applications of the aircraft.

Development of the Boeing also heralded important technical concepts such as Critical Path Analysis and PERT for its initial planning.

Critical Path Analysis is the network analysis technique used to determine the sequence of activities which must be started and finished exactly to plan if the overall project is to be completed to plan. Activities which lie on the critical path must be given more management attention since a delay in any of them will translate into an overall delay of the project. Activities not on the critical path have some 'slack' and can be managed more loosely as long as they are completed to time.

PERT, or Program Evaluation and Review Technique, is a procedure developed in 1958 by the US Navy Special Projects office and the Lockheed Missile and Space division. The PERT approach is 'event-oriented'. The events are defined and connected to show relationships. Each connecting arrow shows precedence and duration of a task.

In a time-scaled diagnosis, the length of the arrows represents the relative time for each activity. The duration is usually expressed as three time estimates for each activity. They are: the pessimistic duration (100 per cent likelihood of missing), the most likely, and the optimistic (100 per cent likelihood of occurring). The calculated duration is then the result of adding the pessimistic duration time to four times the most likely duration time, plus the addition of the optimistic duration time and dividing by 6. Statistical evaluation of the duration in this way allows for determining the probability of meeting any scheduled completion date for a project.

[4]With his feet firmly planted on the factory floor, Fred Carey was fully aware of the problems of integrating companies after a takeover or a merger. After a business is acquired, one of the first detailed tasks is to get the part numbering systems in line with the acquiring organisation since one of the most obvious areas of synergy between businesses is common purchasing. And the key to this are bills of material.

These bills are lists drawn up by the designer specifying the parts, and quantities of those parts, which make up a product or sub-assembly. In addition, they also show how the component parts go into an assembly. Furthermore, bills of material have many uses, including planning for purchasing and manufacturing, product costing and picking materials from stores. They should always represent how the product is manufactured rather than designed and as such they are the prime communication between design and the other functions in the business.

Given the critical importance of bills of material, a series of takeovers or mergers for an engineering company, similar to that which occurred in Britain in the late 1950s and early 1960s, could require major changes to its own existing bills and almost certainly entail wholesale alterations for the companies that were acquired.

Chapter Nine – 1963

*John Kennedy assassinated; First woman in space; John
Profumo resigns; James Dartry becomes chairman of Albion
Engineering*

"This calls for a celebration," Tom Dartry smiled and blew
cigar smoke toward the darkened oak-beamed ceiling of his
Hampshire house. "George, pop downstairs and you'll find a
bottle of '37 port."

"Now you're talking, father!" shouted George, Tom's
younger son, as he darted down to the cellar.

It had been a heady week which began with a hostile bid
for the Albion Engineering Company by its arch rival Empire
Engineering and which ended, today, with the appointment of
Tom's sons, James and George, to the board of Albion. For the
first time in 15 years, a Dartry was in the Albion boardroom
and Tom saw it as the first step to regaining control of a
company that had manifestly lost its way.

Satisfied with their day's work, the three Dartrys now sat
at the dining table, talking and slowly passing the decanter –
filled with 25-year-old port – from one eager hand to another.

James, 27, impeccably dressed and looking very much like
the sharp City businessman he was, fingered his notebook
and inhaled deeply into the crystal port glass. His brother
George, looking more lived-in with a slight air of someone
who had just missed a train, was three years younger than
James but 10 years his junior in business acumen. However,
his slow methodical approach made him an excellent foil to
his brother's more headstrong single-mindedness. Beside the
coal fire, Caesar, the family corgi, lay on his back with all four
paws upright and snarled in his sleep at some imaginary foe.
It was thus an all-male affair. Elinor, Tom's daughter, was still
at college in London whereas Helen, the matriarchal backbone
of the Dartry family, had died the year before.

Tom Dartry leaned across the table. "Tell me again, boys!
From the beginning."

"It was like you said it would be, father," James began. "They were like old Caesar here, just waiting for their tummies to be rubbed. We held all the cards."

In the 15 years since Tom had retired from Albion, the company had grown into a tangled web of incongruous subsidiaries and fringe activities. Some parts were profitable, most were not. It had an annual turnover of more than £95 million and was considered, incorrectly, by many to be a model British engineering company with extensive overseas distribution.

When Albion set up a marine engineering works in the Falkland Islands several years earlier, alarm bells began to ring for Tom and when the company bought a chain of cinemas, he shuddered in disbelief. He worried on two counts: firstly, as the largest shareholder in the company, he feared for the future dividend income his family would receive; secondly, he resented the seemingly incoherent development of a company he had developed on the most rigorous lines of engineering logic.

Then, suddenly on Monday morning, Empire Engineering, his arch rival from the 1930s, had jumped out of the woodwork with its bid. It was a derisory offer – couched in the terms of a friendly merger – and reflected more on how little they could afford to pay for Albion than on how much they thought the company was worth. Tom, now 73, metaphorically sprang into action.

By Monday afternoon, the entire Dartry family of Tom, James, George and Elinor was in the Empire boardroom, sipping sherry and discussing what a merged company would look like. At best, Arthur Woods, septuagenarian chairman of Empire, was offering precisely what they already were in Albion – large silent partners in an unprofitable company. At worst, Tom suspected, they faced extinction.

A rambling tour of Empire's large, gaunt, ugly offices and shop floor confirmed his suspicions. Stocks were high and orders were low. The shopfloor workers that James, George and Elinor had talked to were going on short-time soon. A takeover by Empire was out of the question.

By Wednesday lunchtime, Tom had pledged the support of the Dartry Trust to the Albion board in its defence against

Empire. But there was one condition. His two sons, by now grown men with National Service, university and several years' experience in the City behind them, had to join the Albion board – ostensibly as representatives of the Dartry Trust.

Friday's board meeting confirmed their appointment and the two younger Dartrys made a brief statement of support for the rest of the management and indicated that they wanted to conduct an audit of the company's operations and report back within a month.

This audit began on Friday evening over a bottle of 1937 port.

"Remember your strategy and tactics," Tom admonished his two sons.

"In the UK, we've got six factories. Do you know how many of them make a profit?" he asked.

No, replied both James and George.

"Without looking at the accounts," Tom mused, "I'd guess only two – Mansfield and Luton. And even Luton might be just scraping by. "Scotland never made a penny, it wasn't designed with that in mind. Close it or sell it! Better still, give it to the management, that way you'll have a clear conscience."

George, taken aback by such a suggestion, spoke up: "But father, there'll be so much activity at the new naval bases."

"We're not interested in Faslane or Rosyth," Tom continued. "Trust me. In the long run, the economics are stacked against it. The plant's main market is 400 miles away and transport costs will cripple you in the end."

The same ruthless logic was now applied to the Newcastle plant, which Albion had bought only two years earlier, and then the conversation turned to the Liverpool factory.

"We can't close Liverpool," George said, feeling more confident of his ground. "It's making good money, has been for 10 years."

"Let's listen to father," James suggested.

"Liverpool, on the surface, makes money," Tom began. "But for how long? Its products are dated, the workforce is aging – which means that you have to start hiring young men and train them. Once you do that, you've got them for 25 years. What we need is the right plant producing the right product at the right time in the right location. Scotland, Newcastle and Liverpool don't do that! We can sell Liverpool, maybe to Empire, yes, that's got appeal, but insist on cash, no shares."

Tom passed the port to James.

"Boys, we've always been two companies – one engineering and the other sales. That's been our weakness and strength. I want to be able to look at Albion again and say, yes, it makes bits of planes, armoured cars and household appliances. Try to explain to an investor that we make hydraulic rams in Liverpool, combine harvesters in Rhodesia, diesel engines in Port Stanley and God knows what elsewhere. The company must have logic. We've got to re-establish our chains in the company. It may take years, but it has to be done."

"Pass the port, James," George interrupted, fortifying himself against the picture of all the workers that would have to go.

"You've got to start feeling like owners, not employees," Tom advised. "Build information channels. In the old days, whoever controlled the post bag controlled the company. Letters could go missing, be delayed and that sort of thing. But now you'll have to start looking at computing. See if it can be used in the plant or in the accounts, or for stock control. I think the days of line and balance bin cards are coming to an end."[1]

James passed an empty port decanter to his father as the smoke in the drawing room began to thicken. Another, younger, bottle of port was found and duly gave the three Dartrys new impetus.

"Now for the products!" exclaimed Tom gleefully. "Albion's strategy has become confused. They have the wrong products being made in the wrong places. And probably by the wrong people. We need a modern-day Macready and a Jimmy Fairfax in a room for a week. Then we'd get the right products. It's simply the right mixture of talent and effort.

"Remember what I used to tell you about chains. Design chains. And product chains. How one affects the other. Let's deal with strategy here."

James and George shuffled uneasily in their chairs as they

prepared for another military style approach to business. The port decanter was passed back to James. Tom moved on to a pipe and both his sons lit up American cigarettes.

"You'll have to determine what are the most important products," Tom noted. "This is a strategic decision. Then you have to decide where you make them. At the moment, you have a huge choice of locations, but once you start closing Albion's factories, you'll need to be very careful about your manufacturing location.

"Then you'll need to look at your tactics. Your design tactics should be concerned with the project management of the new designs and modifications. For example, are you going to let engineers work on anything they like, when in fact you should limit the number of projects a person is involved with to a maximum of two.

"Then put some non-technical managers in charge; ex-army types if you like. But don't let the designers keep adding bells and whistles. Insist on them meeting the specification, not exceeding it. Take a look at the PERT idea from the US. Fred Carey knows about it."

James and George looked across the table at each other, a little bit unsure what their father was referring to.

"You should be able to cut down the number of projects under development," Tom continued. "And then some might actually get finished. Then new ideas will get done more quickly. You'll have to rationalise the product range down to a dozen or so basic products."

"But, father," interrupted George, "Albion is making hundreds of products."

"That's right, and that's why the design is so important. You design a product that does the job, and you do it in a way that's easy to make. You think I'm joking? Back in 1944, we had nine torpedo designs with a very high failure rate. We became suspicious of the design. So we tested all the parts individually and they had a near perfect score. But when they were together, something didn't work.

"I told Fred to follow the torpedoes through each stage and watch carefully how they were assembled. Do you know what he saw? Near final assembly, one of our men had to force a small auxiliary motor in through the housing. The opening wasn't big enough. When he did this, he often pulled out some of the wires on the commutator. We were manufacturing duds!"

"Strategically," he continued, "the MoD is a very good customer for Albion, and we should do whatever it takes to make them happy. But don't ignore your other customers. Tactically, you've got to start building your list of civilian customers. The MoD likes to feel that it has you sewn up, that your livelihood depends on them. Give them everything they want, but develop other reliable customers. They'll treat you with more respect that way."

Tom puffed on his pipe thoughtfully, looked at his two sons, and continued.

"After you've closed half the factories and dumped most of the nonsensical products, you've got to sort out your manufacturing tactics. This board has squandered so much buying other companies, I'm certain they haven't invested properly in what they were supposed to. It's as simple as that. Just follow the chains and you'll save the company."

Raising his glass, Tom stood up. James and George did likewise. "Boys," he said, "we've stormed the citadel and they don't even know it yet!"

Within a month, a shell-shocked Albion board accepted a reorganisation plan that disposed of four plants, cut the company's product range by three-quarters, elected James Dartry as their new chief executive and appointed the younger George in the symbolic role of chairman.

Chapter Notes

By the early 1960s, the countries of Western Europe were experiencing an economic boom once again with gross national product two-and-a-half times that of its pre-war level.

Automation and the use of electronic equipment were transforming industry, while chemical research provided an endless variety of synthetic materials. Travel by jet aircraft, one of the final wartime technical innovations, swiftly became a holiday adventure for many whereas television sets emerged as one of the standard features of Western European homes.

Within Britain, nuclear energy had still to live up to its much vaunted promise as a power source for industry although there were hints that the inhospitable North Sea could yield unimaginable sources of energy and industrial feedstock.

In the spirit of the times, Harold Wilson established the Ministry of Technology in 1964, under Frank Cousins and later Tony Benn, to help introduce a 'white hot' technological revolution into British industry. As a government department, it would prove to be confused and extravagant. The Labour government subsequently established the Industrial Reorganisation Corporation to promote 'industrial efficiency and profitability', but this body was in some regards responsible for the flood of mergers that characterised the latter part of the decade.

Reference Notes

[1]Tom Dartry's 14-year 'sabbatical' from Albion gave him the chance to observe many of the new trends that were emerging in British industry. As time marched by, he knew that many old methods of working would need to be discarded. One obvious candidate for replacement was the time-consuming and bureaucratic method of stock control called 'line and balance'. The method required a storeman to record the 'line' number on his stock record and the 'balance', or quantity of inventory which resulted from the transaction, on an authorising document. This document, which might concern a withdrawal, a random issue or an order receipt, was then sent to the inventory controller, who could see instantly if he was missing any transactions. Despite the laborious nature of the method, it none the less worked well and gave high inventory accuracy. In fact, attempts to computerise the method during the 1970s proved unsuccessful and the industry had to wait for the introduction of random perpetual inventory control before it could claim to have a more efficient method of achieving stock accuracy.

Chapter Ten – 1964

Pirate station Radio Caroline starts broadcasting; Première of "A Hard Day's Night"; Richard Burton and Elizabeth Taylor marry

"What sort of woman do you think I am?" joked Elinor Dartry, as she munched on a chocolate biscuit and nursed a half-empty cup of coffee in the college canteen.

"He's the best looking man I've seen this week, just you wait and see," said Katy Baker, Elinor's Russian language classmate. "Totally charming, in an east European sense. I'd put him about ten years older than you – just out of reach."

"Ha! Look who's talking. Anyway, men value experience more than age. I'm certain I exude enough sophistication to turn any man's head, even a visiting lecturer."

"Don't count on it, Elly dear, this one has all you could dream of. Impeccably dressed, even his shoes are polished. When was the last time you saw a pair of polished shoes around here? And he's got impeccable manners. Real traditional stuff, Elly, and speaks a half dozen languages."

"What's his name, Prince Charming?" Elinor mocked.

"No, it's not fairy tale stuff, he's real. A man of the world. His name is Fairfax, Anthony Fairfax."

Elinor's head inclined slightly at the sound of the name.

Anthony Fairfax, only son of James Fairfax, Tom Dartry's original partner in Albion Engineering and Trading Company, strode purposefully in their direction. He was every bit as good looking as Katy had said – tall, slim with beautifully tailored clothes, he did indeed stand out from the more casually and scruffily dressed college students. He stopped on seeing Katy, who introduced him to Elinor.

"Did you say Dartry? Are you related to Sir Thomas Dartry?"

Caught with a mouthful of Kit-Kat, she nodded and muttered the word "Father."

"Then we're related, loosely," Anthony said, "he's my godfather."

Wiping her mouth with a napkin, Elinor's eyes widened in excitement. "I don't believe it!" she gasped. "What other secrets does he have? I know what we'll do, we'll surprise him. Are you free this weekend? Come for afternoon tea on Saturday."

Elinor radiated charm as her fellow student tried to suppress a scowl.

"Well, I haven't seen him in years," Anthony said, "it's too good a chance to miss. I'd be delighted to come. But I must dash now for my next class. You can give me directions later." In an instant the tall, lean, silhouette of Anthony had merged into the shadows of the cold, marbled corridor.

"You're a smooth operator," Katy sneered and pretended to stab Elinor in the chest with her finger. "The dishiest man in college and you invite him to tea!"

"Oh, Katy, stop it. He's family. I thought it would be nice for father."

"And you're the gooseberry?"

"Well, he does seem terribly ... ," she began, but abruptly changed the subject. "Come on, we're late for class."

Breaking into a quick gallop, the two women laughed their way along the echoing hallway and, instead of heading for their scheduled discourse on Slav idioms by Miss Parker, they detoured to Anthony Fairfax's lecture hall where they sat quietly in the back row.

On Saturday afternoon, as Elinor Dartry had forewarned her father, she arrived with an acquaintance from college. When Tom met Anthony in the hall, he could not believe his eyes. Here was a facsimile of his old business partner. And it took Anthony a while to link this frail, slightly stooped, figure with the image of the giant-like man he had seen more than 20 years earlier.

"My word, Elinor, where did you find him?"

"I thought you'd be pleased. When I heard there was a Fairfax in the college, I thought there'd be a connection."

Despite the close family connections, Anthony remained rigidly formal at first. "I am very pleased to meet you again, Sir."

"Rubbish, call me Tom. How's your father?"

"He passed away. Several years ago."

"Oh, Anthony, I'm sorry, I should have known. We really should have kept in touch," Tom said sadly. "He was a unique man, a great man in his own way. Come on, we've got some talking to do."

He led the way into the drawing room while Elinor prepared tea, sandwiches and scones. She could hear them both chattering, occasionally slipping into bouts of laughter. As they came to the tea table, Elinor noted their friendly chat began to resemble more of a cross-examination.

"Your father loved to travel," Tom said in a matter-of-fact way.

"Yes, that's why we moved to Paris. It's central and easier to meet people. I never saw much of father as a teenager, he always seemed to be in faraway places like Bucharest or Istanbul. And, of course, mother died when I was born."

Tom probed. "So why are you in London now?"

"I'm lecturing at the college on East European political frameworks."

Tom Dartry grimaced at the reference to the Eastern bloc.

"A bit specialised, Anthony."

"Yes, I agree. I know very little about political structures per se. Although one can't do business in these countries without understanding the role of the state. As I travel in the region and as I speak Russian and Hungarian they thought I could put some classes together."

Elinor interrupted. "Don't listen to him, father, he knows everything that's going on."

"Elinor is too kind. She exaggerates the importance of a little business acumen and some colourful anecdotes."

She persisted. "Father, he has us spellbound."

"What type of business are you in?" asked Tom.

"Oh, a little bit of import and export, Sir Thomas, nothing very exciting," he replied evasively.

Tom smiled as his mind went back to the 1920s when James Fairfax was also engaged in 'a little bit of import and export'. "Your father loved England so much, he even had a house in Piltdown once."

Anthony nodded in agreement. "Yes, his heart was always in England. But business was elsewhere. He always looked on England as his pole star, his point of reference. I've lived here only a few years but I consider it very much my home."

Unexpectedly, Anthony continued: "The French are quite accommodating to eccentrics, you see. They didn't seem to mind when he built a Tudor house outside Paris. It's quite a well known local attraction and they love the beagles. The French are great dog lovers, just like the English. They were for show really. He liked the idea of looking like a country squire and he so enjoyed the countryside and his English rose garden. 'England', he used to say, 'England is a state of mind. It can be anywhere.' He had the turf for the gardens imported from Folkestone. There were dozens of trucks queueing up to deliver the turf and we had gardeners everywhere laying the lawn. The locals were quite amused by it. As I said, they tolerate eccentrics much more than we do."

While Anthony caught his breath, Tom resumed his probing. "How often are you in England?"

"It depends on the time of year. Perhaps a week every month." Anthony glanced at Elinor pouring the tea. "Some trips can take three months. The bureaucracy in the East is as bad as everyone says it is. Do you manage to travel much?"

"Occasionally, up to London for a dinner or a meeting, but I much prefer to stay in Hampshire," Tom replied.

"Where hurricanes hardly happen," Elinor added jokingly.

"And, of course, I have to keep an eye on my three youngsters."

Elinor baulked. "We are not children, father."

Ignoring her protest, Tom continued. "James is the eldest, 30 or so. Should be around your age, Anthony."

Elinor looked at her tea guest more closely.

"Then there is George, a few years younger and Elinor younger still. None of them married, but all quite prepared to live the bachelor life as far as I can see." Now turning slightly to look Anthony straight in the face, Tom asked if his godson was married.

"Father!" Elinor exploded in exasperation.

"It's all right, Elinor. No, I'm not. Business is a bit too hectic and it wouldn't be fair on the woman or the children. Perhaps in time, but not yet."

He looked at Elinor who blushed and turned away to retrieve the teapot.

For the next hour, godfather and godson chatted about the

burning issues of the day and the trivial things from the past. As the ornate silver clock on the mantelpiece struck five, Tom stood up suddenly. "I've got to be in Salisbury before half-past. Please excuse me, Anthony. Perhaps, I'll see you later." Trying to pre-empt his daughter, Tom raised his voice ever so slightly. "Now Elly, don't fret, I'm all right in the car."

Outmanoeuvred, Elinor tried to get the last word in. "Just cover up well, father."

"Listen to her Anthony. She's behaving like a real mother hen," Tom joked.

Tom gathered his coat and hat from the hallway, bade farewell again and was soon manhandling the veteran Napier down the driveway past Anthony's E-type Jaguar. The spluttering old car was heard in the distance for some time and then all was quiet. Breaking a somewhat awkward silence, Elinor insisted on giving Anthony a tour of the house.

"Oh, Christmas was so much fun here. I used to sneak out of my room on Christmas Eve and watch father and mother place the presents under the tree. They loved it too. Glasses of sherry and mother trying not too hard to escape father's mistletoe. If they saw me watching, they'd get very solemn and tell me about some poor little girl who didn't sleep on Christmas Eve and didn't get presents from Father Christmas. That was enough for me to dash back to bed."

They stood on the three-sided oak-panelled gallery over-looking the drawing room. As Elinor pointed to where her father traditionally placed the family Christmas tree, Anthony reached out and touched her hand. They turned and looked into each other's eyes. They embraced slowly and kissed. And kissed again. For Elinor the world was spinning and the next few steps into her old bedroom seemed the most natural thing in the world. As they later lay in one another's arms, they discovered how easily they chatted and laughed and joked with each other.

As darkness set in, Anthony whispered that he had to leave. They would meet next week at the college. They kissed tenderly and he rose. She heard him leaving through the side door and crunching his way along the gravel driveway past her Mini and into his own car. She lay back in bed, smiled happily and fell asleep.

Their affair, however, proved to be short-lived. When they were together, they loved each other with an intensity that neither thought they possessed. For Elinor each hour, each minute, with Anthony was a joy. The difficult times began as soon as he packed his suitcase and caught a taxi to Heathrow. These business trips were heart-wrenching, bitter, periods for Elinor, who quickly forgot them once Anthony was near her again. However, the trips became longer and more frequent. Even more exotic place names were now peppering Anthony's conversation and, despite suggestions that she join him on some future trips east, Elinor felt they were slipping apart. They simply were not together long enough to make it work out. Finally, after Anthony returned from an extended period in Tashkent, Elinor told him they could not go on like this. She was leaving. Anthony tried to talk to her, promising he would spend more time in England or at least closer to England. It was to no avail.

It was only after they had split up that Elinor discovered she was pregnant. This changed nothing, in her view, other than she would be a mother. And at 24, somewhat younger than she might have wished. Kismet, fate, joss, whatever it was, it was her lot at the moment. Despite pleas from brothers and father alike, Elinor, showing true Dartry obstinacy, steadfastly refused to contact Anthony.

Chapter Eleven – 1969

Neil Armstrong lands on the moon; oil discovered in the North Sea; Willy Brandt elected German Chancellor; "My Way"

An angry George Dartry, nostrils flaring, banged the side of the armoured vehicle with a heavy piece of metal. "This is what engineering is all about!" he shouted above the din of the engineering works. The gaggle of management trainees jumped slightly in shock.

He banged the side of the armoured carrier again. "It's a simple product, with low technology. And it's the result of two chains of activity. I call them product development and product realisation or, in your words, design engineering and manufacturing engineering. By and large, this vehicle is a static product. The only thing that can be improved is the quantity and the efficiency with which we make them. Can we make 14 instead of 13 each week?"

Still seething after a row with his elder brother, George tried to control the tone of his voice in front of the new recruits. But his mind kept returning to the confrontation with James. For the first time in years, George had lost his temper. His brother was increasingly disheartened by what he saw as a lack of spectacular progress, whereas George was content to keep improving what they were doing. James, like an addict hooked on success, needed convincing that he was making the right decisions all the time. He despised failure and he suspected that his father's advice to close their loss-making Scottish plant was flawed. To this end he now proposed to make a strategic move back into Scotland.

The fraternal flare-up occurred when James refused to give more control of the Mansfield and Luton factories to his brother while James was working north of the border. In his eyes, George's role was that of chairman and if he wanted to dabble a bit in the factories, that was fine. But day-to-day control of their production was something else.

What hurt George most was James's unwillingness to

recognise that over the previous five years he had developed into an effective manager, capable of running complex production programmes and at the same time to second-guess the competition successfully. These were five years James now claimed had been wasted.

Wasted or not, they had seen Albion Engineering, since renamed AEL, follow the blueprint set out by their father. Factories were closed, workers redeployed, and the product range cut drastically. A company once employing 2,200 now had 800 workers. Profitability improved and AEL, while still controlling valuable shares of the household appliance and low-technology defence equipment markets, began to move into some new areas such as missile guidance systems. Yet something was wrong. They were in the right markets and were working on key contracts. It simply came down to the fact that they weren't doing their job terribly well.

At times like this, George wished he had Fred Carey working along side him. Fred had been active in AEL up to a few years earlier but suffered a stroke in early 1968 and died shortly afterwards. As a mark of respect, James and George closed the Mansfield factory for a day so that the workforce could attend his funeral.

Shortly after Fred's death, as Elinor Dartry struggled to raise her four-year-old daughter amid rioting students in Paris, George decided there was a gap, a missing link if you like, in their approach to the business. His father, quietly watching from the sidelines, readily agreed that strategy and tactics were only the starting point for his theory on engineering, that other dimensions to the design and manufacturing chains could exist.

Now looking at his group of trainees, George decided the time was ripe to hoist the flag.

Armed with a piece of chalk, George wrote the words PRODUCT DEVELOPMENT on the left rear door of the armoured vehicle and PRODUCT REALISATION on the right hand door. He underlined both.

Pointing to PRODUCT DEVELOPMENT, he began. "In my father's day, somebody decided it was strategically important to make 500-pound bombs instead of 250-pound bombs. That's a simple strategic decision which sets the chain in motion. He did something similar with washing machines, but that's another story."

He wrote S*TRATEGIC* on the door.

"Once the strategy is decided, tactics come into play in designing the product. This is straightforward, using the best available methods to design a product."

George wrote T*ACTICAL* under S*TRATEGIC*.

"He used simple systems and tools like slide rules and log tables.We might use computers with sophisticated finite element programmes to help but, like any other tool, you use them to do a job at the right time.[1]

George pointed again to T*ACTICAL* and continued.

"Technical people always seem to do things in sequence. We also discovered it's more effective to get our designers working in a team in the same place. There's no point in having half the team in Newcastle and the other half in Mansfield. It boils down to simple tactics."

Now under P*RODUCT* R*EALISATION*, he now wrote S*TRATEGIC*.

"After design, you have to make the product – you need to decide the best trade-off between manufacturing scale and your distribution network.

"During the war, the government insisted on a plant in Scotland. It served its purpose – it was never bombed, but it lost money every day of its life after 1945."

T*ACTICAL* was now written on the door of the vehicle.

"Having decided that one, two, or three factories is the optimum, you now have to optimise what you do in each of them. This means optimising inventory and achieving the best lead times possible.

"So far so good. But I'm convinced there's more to it than this. If you want a good company, there's another link in both of these chains."

He wrote O*PERATIONAL* in large block capital letters.

"Both chains have an operational dimension. Tom Dartry wasn't too concerned about waste in design or manufacturing, provided it was kept within a manageable level. He wasn't, but I am. We simply cannot afford waste materials or lost machine time through poor scheduling. [2]

"In product design, the O*PERATIONAL* phase is difficult to define. It has to do with quality or robustness. A raincoat is supposed to keep out the rain. If it doesn't, then you're entitled to your money back."

Tapping the word OPERATIONAL, he went on: "Let's look at how this affects the product realisation chain. This simply means making the goods better and cutting out waste wherever possible. Look at that wheel on the Leyland transporter. Now look at our armoured carrier. What's the difference?"

A hesitant voice was heard from the middle of the group.

"You're right. Each Leyland wheel has 10 nuts holding it onto the axle. We use five. We designed it originally with 10, because we were concerned about safety. but it was simple overspecification. We'd be perfectly safe with four, and in an emergency, two would be enough. We know because we've tested it. Who needs 10?"

"Then why are there five?" asked one of the bolder management trainees.

"Military men get a bit anxious if they see things cut right back. So we used five nuts instead of four, and we've welded a couple of spares onto the inside panels of the vehicle. You can knock them off with a spade. Now the vehicle looks safer than before, even though there's only half the wheel nuts. This is where the two chains overlap. Design efficiency leads to manufacturing efficiency."

For dramatic effect, he banged each word on the doors with a metal bar:

PRODUCT DEVELOPMENT	PRODUCT REALISATION
STRATEGIC	STRATEGIC
TACTICAL	TACTICAL
OPERATIONAL	OPERATIONAL

"Any questions?"

Emboldened by the earlier question, another trainee asked: "Isn't the factory a link in both chains?"

George smiled. "Well done," he said, "You've grasped the idea. Yes, the factory is a link in both. That's exactly why it's so difficult to work in manufacturing and so exciting when things go right."

With his OPERATIONAL phase of the chain now completely

out in the open and his brother more or less resigned to his greater involvement in AEL, George began putting theory into practice. His goal was simply to improve the operational efficiency of everything they did. He began to visit other engineering companies such as Rolls-Royce to 'borrow' some of their ideas and see how they approached common problems.[3] Rolls' experience with computers spurred him on to look at other ways of coping with the planning of materials[4] and quality by using techniques like statistical process control.[5] He quickly developed an obsession with numerical control, or NC, technology.[6] Over several months, George saw the first signs that parts of AEL were responding to his new treatment. He didn't expect a sudden outburst of productivity, but would settle for a gentle flicker of life at first, confirming that something new was stirring in the corporate soul.

As George was working on improving the operational efficiency of the company, James embarked on what he hoped would be a strategic move by AEL into new markets. He had agreed reluctantly to cede *de facto* day-to-day control of the business to George and appointed him Operations Director in order to focus on his own Scottish strategy. He now found himself sitting in a London hotel suite listening to the rapid-fire monologue of an Oklahoma oilman who had a small stake in a North Sea oil exploration consortium. Sitting opposite him was Litton Malone, one of the last of a dying breed of high-risk, high-reward oilmen who would stake everything on a hunch. Malone's unconventional entry to the North Sea was through a small, speculative company called Orion Services which acted as a bridge between large operators and local pools of expertise. He bartered small stakes in Orion for engineering and supply services. For everyone, the attraction, the lure, was millions of barrels of oil.

"Some of our engineering work has to be done in Oklahoma," Malone explained. "That's part of the deal I've already done with some friends, but the quick stuff can be done in England or Scotland or god knows where. Just so long as we get good back-up."

Malone now made his pitch: for a half million dollars' worth of support engineering, he was prepared to give AEL 25 per cent of his stake. "You meet your cash calls on that share," he explained, "and then chip in whatever engineering work is needed to keep the whole thing going."

"Sounds fair. What happens if you don't meet your own cash calls?" asked James.

"My holding is diluted. If you meet them for me, your holding is increased. Well, what's your answer?"

"Yes, provided my board agrees."

"Now, you're talking Dartry. Not enough of that around this town," Malone grunted. He stubbed his cigar into the ashtray and shook James's hand firmly.

In effect, AEL had bought a 1.25 per cent stake in an exploration consortium that was operating in some of the most difficult conditions in the North Sea. Gas had already been discovered in the more docile southern portion of the North Sea during the mid-1960s, but now the hunt moved to higher latitudes.

Prospects of discovering commercial quantities of oil were considered reasonable, but many companies were staggered at the enormous costs of even a small exploration programme and any subsequent development work. No one had ever worked in such hostile waters where appalling weather could make even the simplest task almost impossible to complete.

James likened the deal to having an option on a 10ft x 10ft plot of land in Piccadilly Circus or Times Square. With so much drilling going on in the area, as soon as someone struck oil, his minuscule stake would soar in value. Although not a gambler by nature, James had to admit that the oil business had a lot of adrenalin coursing through its veins.

For James, exposure to the oil industry was an eye-opener. Many of the niceties of traditional English commerce were cast out the window. At times he felt he was dealing with horse traders, but he also sensed he was dealing with men of honour. His vocabulary was suddenly enlarged to include colourful terms like Christmas trees, pigs and weather windows. Geological nomenclature like Jurassic and Palaeozoic were suddenly recovered from his school days and pressed into action.

To meet the engineering demands of Orion, James set up within the Mansfield factory a small dedicated office, which he staffed with a handful of his most experienced men. The early, spring months of the new operation were fine. Orion would call the office to warn of impending problems and the office, in turn, would reserve the necessary capacity in the plants. Oilfield work took priority over everything else, much to the consternation of some old hands who moaned about the constant set-ups needed for the specialist repairs.

Drilling rigs work 24 hours a day, seven days a week. If a spare part is not available, things can literally grind to a halt. To meet this demand, the Mansfield office was manned from 7 am to 11 pm, after which calls were switched through to the manager's home.

At about 4 am on a blustery Sunday morning in August, James was rudely awakened by the endless ringing of his telephone downstairs. It was an irate Litton Malone, who, telephoning from Aberdeen, began to heap abuse on James and AEL.

"Damn it, man, this is a 24-hour show, we don't keep office hours in the North Sea. We've got an emergency and I want back-up. That sonofabitch manager of yours isn't answering the phone. We're busting our balls just trying to keep the show on the road, and you lot are tucked up warm in bed. Start kicking ass, James, or pack your bags!" Malone hung up.

James was left speechless. Chains, chains everywhere. He now saw himself as the weakest link in Malone's engineering chain in the North Sea, and he hated himself for it. Something would have to be done urgently. He quickly dressed and drove over to the house of his duty manager. It took the sleepy-eyed man a while to recognise James in the poor light of the porchway. Once inside, James conducted a thorough, if somewhat rude, probe into the man's previous few hours. No, there had not been any telephone calls. Of course, he would check the phones. In the event, there appeared to be a line fault which allowed only outgoing calls. Now to smooth James's evidently ruffled feathers, he drove down to the Albion works depot, contacted Malone by telex and promised the maverick oilman that the parts he needed would be with him by lunchtime.

Once the emergency was over, James pondered how to avoid similar near-misses in the future, not only with Malone but with other customers. He began to visit Edinburgh and

Aberdeen more regularly. At first, these one-day sorties were sufficient to follow the progress of other small engineering supply companies and to keep the AEL flag flying, but longer trips soon became necessary.

After a year of shuttling to the North Sea, James began to see progress in establishing the company's reputation. Such glimmers of success energised him and, in the words of one City observer, he was now deemed to be 'a young man in a hurry'. There was also a change of atmosphere in the City where such young men were more than tolerated, they were now positively encouraged.

The mood in the Square Mile mirrored a wider change in Britain. Unemployment had broken through the one million barrier for the first time in memory and the Heath government was stoking up the economy. Controls on credit and banking were relaxed, triggering a speculative property boom and a stock market rally. Runaway inflation fuelled industrial unrest across the country and the first significant strike was organised by the miners in February 1972. Suddenly, British industry was placed on a three-day working week to save fuel. In James's absence, George called a crisis meeting of the board to consider their strategy during the strike.

Almost twitching with excitement, George outlined a bold plan. Of course, they would accept the government's three-day week. But he didn't want to lose any production! Several members of the board baulked at the suggestion and said it was unreasonable in the circumstances.

"This strike is not a catastrophe, it's the opportunity I've been looking for. Don't you see, it's the OPERATIONAL phase of the chain. We have a chance to boost productivity for three days of the week. If we can squeeze five days' output from three working days, that means we're 40 per cent inefficient. Let's see how efficient we really are!"

"From today," he announced flatly, "AEL operates a permanent three-day week regardless of when the strike is settled."

By early March, the miners' strike was over. Industry had faced just 20 days of power cuts. Few took notice of AEL's continued three-day week, and when they did, they assumed it was due to a thin order book. Within AEL, the shopfloor workers, long encouraged to seek shorter working hours, seemed content with their three 12-hour shifts, which still allowed scope for extra overtime.

At the same time, George was conscious of the impression City investors and analysts might make of his permanent short-time working. Seizing the initiative, he organised a series of lunches for London brokers and institutional investors at which he suggested to his guests that if they wished to consider AEL an anomaly, they should consider them an efficient one. Driving the point home in the only language they understood, he revealed that profits for the coming year would be 18 per cent higher because operating costs had been slashed by more than a third.

And so AEL went on. Clawing back productivity, investing in new technology and building up earnings. City analysts and investors were content to let sleeping dogs lie as the Dartrys seemed to be in control of what they were doing. As long as the company was making good profits, they were not overly concerned about the seemingly bottomless pit of investment in the North Sea.

By mid-summer 1973, at the height of the North Sea drilling season, AEL received a coded telex message from James in Aberdeen. Traces of oil had been found at an unexpected depth. It could be a small pinched reservoir not worth bringing into production or it could be the first signs of a lucrative pay-zone. More drill tests were conducted. Further drilling took place. As the weather window began to close, a second rig was hired to fathom the extent of the discovery. Then suddenly, *Bonanza!* It was officially declared a medium-sized field of high quality oil with substantial associated gas, close to the larger Forties and Argyll fields.

An ebullient James telexed his brother: HELLO MANSFIELD, GREETINGS FROM TIMES SQUARE!

James's timing, or luck, was impeccable. AEL was now a part-owner – admittedly, at 1.25 per cent a very small part-owner – of an oilfield that would generate millions of pounds in profit for the next 30 years. Within months, the importance of this postage stamp of North Sea acreage would escalate even further in value.

By October, the Middle East was at war and Opec stunned

the world with crude oil prices rises of 70 per cent. The first global oil shock had arrived and the race was on to land North Sea oil on British soil as quickly as possible.

To this end, AEL pushed its engineering capabilities to the limit. George's OPERATIONAL phase of the chain was now producing dramatic results. Output was rising and operational costs were falling as both Mansfield and Luton were working to maximum capacity. He now felt confident to invest heavily in new NC milling machinery to give the company fresh scope for boosting output. To cope with the further production that James now needed, George reluctantly agreed to reinstitute a four-day working week, but only on condition he could be guaranteed a one-third jump in production. In time, as news of its North Sea discovery filtered into the popular tabloid press, AEL was somewhat mislabelled as the 'oil-rich buggers on a four-day week'.

James now permanently based himself in Aberdeen and, apart from servicing Litton Malone's needs, began to pick up other valuable engineering work. By late 1974, as the North Sea weather steadily worsened, he was commuting across the highlands and lowlands of Scotland, examining sites for building offshore production platforms, storage terminals and supply bases.

One afternoon, he was due to meet Malone aboard the drilling rig *Marine Star* for a late meeting. The helicopter flight plan included a detour to the Orkneys to look at Occidental's proposed site for an oil storage facility at Flotta, which looked northward onto Scapa Flow, where the German High Seas fleet was scuttled after the First World War.

From the deck of Malone's rig, the helicopter was seen approaching slightly off-course due to high winds. It then appeared to lose height and smoke was seen coming from its engine. Crew aboard the *Marine Star* signalled the alarm just as the Sikorsky hit the water and turned upside down like a turtle.

Of two crew and six passengers, only one survived. The body of James Dartry was among those recovered from the scene of the crash.

Chapter Notes

At the start of the 1970s, the technological capability of advanced industrial nations appeared limitless. Successful lunar landings by the US illustrated quite dramatically how engineering, when backed by lavish government budgets, could overcome fundamental hurdles such as space travel. In Europe, time and space had also been tamed, albeit more modestly, with the Anglo-French supersonic Concorde programme.

Accompanying this newly found faith in engineering was an important shift in the political predisposition of Britain. In fact at the beginning of the decade, Britain had accepted the reality of the rapidly improving political and economic situation in continental Europe. Under the premiership of Edward Heath, the Conservative government had concluded that its future lay with cultivating their continental connections rather than trying to maintain a 'special relationship' with the US or the Commonwealth. In time, Britain's membership of the EEC, effective from 1973, would prompt it to refocus its political and commercial efforts towards its European partners.

Politics apart, British industry was also undergoing a major transformation at this time. The merger trend of the late 1960s and subsequent waves of takeovers had produced a new cluster of diversified companies or conglomerates. These corporate goliaths claimed that through 'synergy' or 'economies of scale' they would operate more efficiently. Every merger was heralded as promoting efficiency and enhancing future profitability but many, particularly in the brewing, hotels, armaments and light engineering industries, turned out to be less efficient than their former constituent parts. By the mid-1970s, many conglomerates were, in fact, less profitable than those companies that had remained independent. As unemployment accelerated through the decade, it became apparent that most of these trail-blazing companies, which were constantly increasing their ratio of capital to labour, were actually cutting jobs instead of creating additional employment.

Reference Notes

[1]At this stage, George Dartry was quite ambitious in suggesting that AEL could use finite element programmes, especially since they

were only viable when a computer with a sufficiently large memory was available.

Notwithstanding this, the finite element method, developed by Professor O.C. Zienkiewicz at Swansea University, made use of approximating numerical functions to solve a range of engineering problems. The method entails a grid array of small, usually identical, sample elements in a model. The nodes or points at which the elements meet are then used to find solutions for the many individual elements which make up the model.

[2]A crucial feature within the Dartry Chain was the reduction or elimination of waste at every stage of the engineering process. Consequently, machine scheduling, or deciding which parts to process in the queue for a machine, was one of the first, and historically one of the most intractable, areas that came under close scrutiny.

Intuitively, it should be easy to find a mathematical solution to the problems in production control. However, there has been only one specified case, known as Johnston's Rule, where a mathematical optimum solution has been determined. In all other cases, every possible combination of sequences or schedules must be examined to find the optimum. The difficulty rapidly grows out of proportion with the problem. For example, with just 20 machines and 20 jobs, it would take more than a century on the world's fastest computer to examine every possible production schedule. Production controllers, therefore, use heuristic rules, or rules of thumb, to determine schedules. They assume generally that the capacity of a machine is infinite and sequence the work queues on the basis of some rule such as first-in first-out or earliest due date.

[3]In George's eyes, Rolls-Royce was by now at the cutting edge of British engineering technology. In fact, the production control computer system called MAGPIE that Rolls-Royce introduced in the late 1960s was the first integrated materials management system. Designed by D. Esse, it operated in batch mode but had most of the functions of later, more sophisticated, computer systems.

George's near blind faith in Rolls-Royce took a severe pounding when this doyen of British engineering came close to destruction with the celebrated RB211 programme. By attempting to achieve a quantum leap in technology, R-R misjudged the huge development costs of the aero-engine and the British government, in a desperate bid to save the company, was forced to nationalise it in November 1970. The company was eventually re-privatised by the Thatcher government in 1986.

[4]Studying Rolls-Royce's materials management system led George naturally to examine AEL's existing method of ordering materials. Up to this stage, he had used the order point method, which required a trigger point to be established based on the average use of a component. When this point was reached, a new order would be initiated. There were, however, obvious disadvantages to this method when customer demand was changing rapidly, when new products were introduced or old products were discontinued.

As for critical components, it was normal practice to calculate their requirements over a period of 13 weeks from a finished product forecast and the bills of material. Given that this process was inordinately time-consuming, it was conducted only four times a year. However, by the early 1970s, as computer capabilities increased, such tasks previously performed by hand were automated and conducted more frequently. The practice then acquired its popular name Material Requirements Planning (MRP), which in turn led to Manufacturing Resource Planning, or MRP II.

[5]Central to George's crusade against waste was the concept of manufacturing quality products in the first place. By the start of the 1970s, normal practice in a machine shop was to run a few components off after a machine was reset and then to check them thoroughly. If the inspection proved satisfactory, production would proceed.

A more methodical approach entails Statistical Process Control (SPC). With this technique, first proposed by Dr Walter Shewhart at Bell Laboratories in the 1920s, a machine or process is examined at a specified time interval and a random sample of items is selected from a recently-produced batch. Points are then plotted on a SPC chart. Normally, there are inner and outer control lines on the chart. If the plotted point is below both of these control lines no action need be taken. On the other hand, if two consecutive plotted points are between the control lines then action is taken to determine whether a fault has entered the engineering process. If a point is beyond the control lines then the process is stopped immediately. It is normal practice to set the outer control limit so that only 1 per cent of production, or 3.09 standard deviations, will normally fall outside the limit under normal conditions.

By the 1980s, several companies, including Motorola, introduced SPC programmes that tolerated only one part in 10 million to fall outside the control lines.

[6]George Dartry instinctively saw numerical control machine technology as a further method of improving AEL's engineering quality. NC technology entails the control of production equipment in real time through pre-recorded symbolic instructions. Instead of a person operating a machine, a set of prepared instructions are used and decoded by the machine causing it to operate. Though the technology is applied to a wide variety of production equipment, the term numerical control in general is used to refer to machine tools only.

Developed in the 1950s by the Massachusetts Institute of Technology under a contract from the US Air Force, early NC machines used handwired logic circuits with punched paper tapes as the instruction media. Subsequent development of direct numerical control (DNC) eliminated the use of paper tapes as each machine was connected to a host computer and the part program sent to the machine in real time.

With the advent of microprocessors, computer numerical control (CNC) was developed and NC machines were equipped with microprocessor-based controllers, local memory and input devices. CNC eliminated the problem of worn punched tape and dependency on a host computer.

CNC machines were quickly followed by distributed numerical control systems (also abbreviated to DNC, and thereby causing some ambiguity). With distributed NC technology, CNC machines are tied to a host computer which provides a central storage site for programs that are downloaded to machines for execution.

Chapter Twelve – 1979

The Shah of Iran flees Tehran; BL stops production of the MG; oil prices soar; the Conservatives win the UK general election

The waiter, ram-rod straight, appeared at the table with a grim demeanour. Elinor Dartry was the last to notice him.

"Miss Dartry, there is an urgent telephone call. Would you like to take it here?"

Somewhat startled, Elinor's mind jumped to a thousand and one conclusions simultaneously. "My god, what's wrong? Yes, of course."

She picked up the handset: "George? Are you all right? What's happened?"

An exuberant George Dartry was telephoning from London: "Elly, I'm fine. She's done it. You're on your way. It's now or never."

"Have you been drinking?" she asked in a harsh parental tone.

"Don't be silly. Haven't you heard the result? She's done it. The first woman in British politics. Thatcher has won!"

Elinor still failed to grasp the significance of her brother's news. "That's marvellous George, but I never vote Tory, you know that."

"Listen to me! Now is the time. Get back quickly. You're about to take over AEL. The waiting is over. Congratulations!" George then hung up.

Appearing slightly flustered and just beginning to realise the impact of the call, Elinor pushed the telephone away and sank back into her chair. One of her dinner companions at the Massachusetts Institute of Technology asked if she were all right.

Looking a little dazed, she responded, "Yes, I'm fine. I've had some strange news from London. Margaret Thatcher has been elected prime minister."

"A woman prime minister?" joked one of the businessmen at Elinor's table. "Wonders never cease. Could you pass the salt, please?"

Shortly after the death of her brother in 1974, 33-year-old Elinor had returned to the fold. Her estrangement and, following the birth of her daughter, the collapse of a promising career in scientific research, were in the past. From 1974 onwards, she began to make up lost ground in the family business.

She was tutored by her father in the theory and practice of the Dartry chains and quickly blended into the background at AEL. Disillusioned in love – she seldom saw Anthony Fairfax again, and had it not been for her daughter Elena she would have doubted whether he had ever existed – Elinor threw herself into her job.

She helped her father rummage through the old Albion storeroom in Queen Street, which had miraculously escaped bombardment in the war and even more incredibly had survived the post-war reconstruction frenzy that had gripped the City.

Elinor sensed the importance of their work to her father. They grew close, perhaps for the first time in their lives. Don't be impatient, he counselled, your time will come. Interesting advice, she thought, from a man in his early eighties. But she relented. For the moment, at least. She was prepared to wait to see what fate would deliver to her. But in the meantime, her father insisted, she had to understand more about manufacturing processes and plumb the depths of modern management thinking. And George, who had succeeded his late brother as chief executive of AEL as well as retaining his roles of chairman and operations director, insisted she join the board.

So it went on. For years. Waiting. Although her time was frustrating, it was not unproductive. She learned quickly and displayed the Dartry family trait of a good memory. Eventually, by the time her father died in 1976, she was one of the most competent, and underestimated, directors of the company.

Tom Dartry's death at the age of 86 marked the passing of an era. He had been found, with a copy of the 1948 accounts on his lap, slumped in a large wing-back chair in the boardroom. His obituary in *The Times* referred to his early years in the Royal Engineers Signal Service and his contribution to war production during the Second World War. For the family, and the company, though, he had moved against the tide of history by creating a modern approach to engineering. AEL's 1,200 employees had something to be proud of.

For Elinor, however, her father's death appeared to change nothing in the company. Still she waited. But now less willing to accept the second-class citizenship she had been granted, she surreptitiously visited parts of the works she had never seen before. She donned blue overalls and joined delivery men on their rounds. She turned up to work beside the tea ladies, the post boy, the central buyer, the chief storeman, the hapless team of amateurs trying to install a new computer system, the accountant and the auditors. No one questioned her, no one needed to.

In the summer of 1978 after another year of working her way through AEL, Elinor and her daughter went on a camping holiday to Cornwall. A week later, she stood in front of George and, sticking her toe into the deep shag pile carpet on his office floor, took a deep breath. "There has been a communications breakdown between design and manufacturing."

"What are you talking about?"

"The chain is broken. Don't you see?" she persisted.

"So we'll fix it, Elly, we've fixed it in the past," George said a little too dismissively for Elinor's liking

"It's more fundamental than that. I need to show you some charts I've drawn up. We have four major factors to worry about in the company. Quality, Delivery, Service and Price..."

"Stop! Elly, I don't think I follow you. What are you getting at and what does it have to do with our chains?"

"I think I've found another level, another way to look at the chains."

"If you've done that, well done."

"Don't patronise me, George, I've had enough of that for a lifetime!"

George relented. "Oh, calm down Elly and tell me."

She began: "We know all about the strategic and tactical aspects of our manufacturing chain. And we've been doing good work on the operational."

Now George felt he was losing patience. "Yes, Elly, get on with it."

On a large flip-chart, she drew a line and every few inches she placed the date of a decade beginning with the 1920s. At the bottom left-hand margin, she wrote FINANCIALS, which she defined as turnover, profit, dividend, return on capital. "We know what these are from our annual accounts, whether they have been good or bad," she said.

Further along the margin she wrote the words QUALITY, DELIVERY, SERVICE and PRICE. "These are the attributes of a good company from the point of view of a customer."

The outline looked like this:

	1920s	1930s	1940s	1950s	1960s	1970s	1980s
QUALITY DELIVERY SERVICE PRICE FINANCIALS	Good	Bad	Good	Good	Bad	Bad	?

"Is this worth the analysis?" asked George severely.

Undeterred, Elinor continued. "Just wait until we start filling in the gaps, and you'll see what happens. Broadly speaking, quality as an attribute of the company has not always been a predominant factor in our lives. Certainly, it was during the war, and has been during the last couple of years. Let's fill these in with an X. If we do the same for delivery, we'd probably need Xs in the 1920s, part of the 1960s and some recent years. So now, the scheme starts to look like this...''

	1920s	1930s	1940s	1950s	1960s	1970s	1980s
QUALITY			X		X		?X
DELIVERY	X				X		?X
SERVICE							
PRICE							
FINANCIALS	Good	Bad	Good	Good	Bad	Bad	?

"When we plot the service element on the chart, we see how important it has been over the decades," she explained. "We need to place Xs during the 1930s, the 1950s, and now 1977. Our customers have always expected high levels of service!"

George nodded in agreement.

	1920s	1930s	1940s	1950s	1960s	1970s	1980s
QUALITY			X		X		?X
DELIVERY	X				X		?X
SERVICE		X		X		X	?X
PRICE							
FINANCIALS	Good	Bad	Good	Good	Bad	Bad	?

"And finally, price. Price has been important recently and was important during the 1930s, So let's put a few Xs there. So our chart begins to look like this..."

	1920s	1930s	1940s	1950s	1960s	1970s	1980s
QUALITY			X		X		?X
DELIVERY	X				X		?X
SERVICE		X		X		X	?X
PRICE		X				X	?X
FINANCIALS	Good	Bad	Good	Good	Bad	Bad	?

"We don't just have to limit ourselves to these four attributes," she explained, "but I think they are the important ones for customer satisfaction. We could look at internal things like design, number of new products, quality of labour and almost anything you like. What do you think?"

"All this shows me is that things have got tougher in the last sixty years. I'm sorry, Elly, no points for that."

"You don't understand. In fact it's so simple, it's easy to miss. What's the most obvious thing about this sketch?"

"It covers 60 years."

"Yes. That's it. This is the history of AEL, or maybe of British industry over the past 60 years," she said triumphantly. "The key is time. Things change through time. There's no point in being good at something if the market wants something else. We must change with the market, we must look at the company continuously. The fourth dimension of the chain is time. We must find shortcomings in what we do presently, and learn to do them better. The main point is that over time, the emphasis within the company shifts. And the demands made on it from outside also shift."

At last, George began to understand his sister's reasoning. "Are you serious about this. How did you come across it?"

"From sitting with father and listening to him. It wasn't until I saw the company in detail did I see how important it was. This dimension could be called CONTINUOUS REVIEW, where we constantly examine all the elements of our strategy, tactics and operational efficiency. It's as obvious as the nose on my face."

Elinor's formulation of a fourth link in the Dartry chains was the psychological breakthrough she had so desperately needed. From that day, George took her very seriously as a businesswoman. His unspoken aim was for her to succeed him as chairman and chief executive. But like his father, he realised that the time for her succession was not right. In the interim, however, Elinor's board position was strengthened by her appointment as director of planning with responsibility for a small team of experts looking at the complete overhaul of AEL's business strategy.

Elinor's CONTINUOUS dimension prompted some critical re-examination of the company's projects. In a master stroke of crossbreeding of ideas, Elinor packed a mundane washing machine full of electronic circuitry from a missile and created a new generation of household appliances in the process. Bosch, AEG, even Electrolux, were stopped in their tracks.

The success of the washing machine programme convinced George that Elinor had the vision which AEL would need for the future. He decided that when the time was right – he was a bit vague as to what this meant precisely – he would step aside and give Elinor free rein, although he would remain sufficiently in the foreground as chairman of AEL to allay outside fears. But he was quite certain that Elinor would have full control of the company one day.

That day had now arrived with the election of Margaret Thatcher in May 1979. It would herald the new age of businesswomen, the female managing director. Immediately after taking George's late night call from London, Elinor booked onto the first available flight to Heathrow. By early evening the next day, she and George were bumping along the M4 to Hampshire in the 50-year-old family Napier, which had recently undergone a major overhaul in Mansfield and which was regularly wheeled out on important ceremonial occasions. This was deemed to be such an occasion.

George told his sister how the City had breathed a sigh of relief at the Conservative victory and how the country seemed prepared for a new era. He also outlined his immediate tactics for dealing with AEL's board and, true to his word, embarked on a series of telephone calls as soon as he arrived at the house. A carefully concocted mixture of promises and blunt threats to the board was sufficient to stifle any internal opposition to her appointment although his manoeuvres were greeted with mild disbelief by the City, which baulked at the notion of family dynasties in public companies.

Some clever financial engineering, which might enable the doubling the dividend to ordinary shareholders for the next two years, helped the investment community see Elinor's appointment in a new light. George hoped the thinly-veiled bribery – funded by an acceleration of their oil producing stake in the North Sea – would give her the breathing space she needed to get established.

As well as giving Elinor the time she needed, George gave her plenty of sound advice about her board of terrified misogynists. Sitting with his feet up on the dining table, George called across the room to his sister. "They understand the subtlety of a tank and you need the manners of an SAS hit team. In other words, Elly, no points for being nice."

"Oh, George! What if they don't take me seriously?" Elinor seemed genuinely worried.

"Sack them," George shouted to her.

"I can't do that!" she shouted back.

"And why not?"

"Well, I can't," Elinor replied somewhat lamely.

"Then delegate. If that doesn't work, then sack them!" They both laughed.

Elinor now moved closer to her brother and asked, perhaps for the fiftieth time, why he was giving up something he enjoyed so much.

"I'm not giving up anything," he joked. "Just redistributing the power. In truth, I'm tired. Tired of doing both jobs and tired of keeping my eye on too many balls at the same time. The company has grown too large for me. You're fresher, you've got new ideas and a different outlook. But tell me, Elly, what is the first thing you really want to do with the company?"

Looking across the room, she replied, more to the walnut panelling than to her brother: "Something no other Dartry has tried. I want to take over Empire Engineering!"

"You see, I'm right!"

Chapter Notes

The 1980s were the age of big business and saw the advent of the Yuppie, mobile telephones, insider trading, green mail, leveraged buyouts and junk bonds.

In Britain, the 1979-81 period was one of savage recession which eroded much of the country's industrial base. In time, this economic downturn would give way to new booming financial markets and service industries that on the face of it appeared to repair much of the damage caused by the earlier recession. In due course, this frenetic boom of the mid-1980s would be followed by another, more serious, recession at the end of the decade that further cut into the manufacturing capability of British industry, a trend that would spill over into the early 1990s.

However, as a period of modern British life, the 1980s would always be inextricably linked with Margaret Thatcher. This crusader of free enterprise, popular capitalism and the emasculation of trade unions would attempt to create a new political and economic renaissance in Britain. Notwithstanding some major achievements, she would resign as prime minister in November 1990 amid Conservative Party in-fighting over Britain's role in European affairs. And as Britain slumped into its third recession in 20 years, Thatcher's policies would prove increasingly difficult for her successors to pursue.

Chapter Thirteen – 1981

Iran releases US hostages; Prince Charles marries Lady Diana Spencer; Norman Tebbitt urges British unemployed to 'get on their bikes' and look for work

By 10.05 am, it was over. Empire Engineering, once doyen of the British industrial might, ceased to exist.

The dawn raid had started a few minutes after the opening of the London Stock Exchange and block trades of 400,000, 250,000 and 300,000 shares had signalled to the rest of the market that Empire was under attack and, so evidently lacking institutional support, was deemed dead in the water.

Elinor had prepared her attack well and, with the aid of brokers Boyd & Benson, met little opposition. She had concluded, rightly, that few rivals would be prepared to go beyond her generous offer as none had the same unusual mix of nostalgia and vendetta for Empire.

But there were two simple factors operating in her favour. Firstly, by the time she launched her bid, Britain's entire engineering sector was stumbling along trying to fend off cut-throat foreign competition and a government intent on forcing industrial discipline on a reluctant workforce. Secondly, AEL, unlike its impoverished competitors, had a steady flow of North Sea oil revenue into its accounts.

By 11 o'clock, she addressed a meeting of the AEL board to tell them that the much-vaunted and often delayed bid had been a success. For £6.2 million, they now owned an unusual collection of industrial enterprises, and one of the great names in British engineering. It was time to get to work, she instructed the board. Like a well-rehearsed act, the board moved into action. Elinor knew she would need to make decisions quickly about some of the odder bits of Empire and the only way this could be done was by getting reliable information out of the company swiftly.

Empire, by now, was a loose amalgam of engineering companies which had evolved haphazardly over the previous four decades. The discipline of war-time production had been swiftly replaced by a manic willingness to produce anything for anyone. A product range, swollen by military needs, had been extended even further. Whereas a handful of motor designs may have existed previously, two dozen now cluttered up the warehouse and assembly lines. While some of the company's plants were efficient and well-run, others were embroiled in labour disputes over union recognition and pay. Output, profits, and morale among its 1,300 workers had all hit rock bottom.

Elinor's approach to this hodge-podge was simple. She seconded George and two others from the AEL board to go into Empire on the day of the takeover with instructions to see what was salvageable and what had to go. George likened the experience to being dropped behind enemy lines and feeding battle data back to the Albion HQ.

At the end of the first day, Elinor sat with her brother and tried to smother a sense of excitement. She felt as though she had been given the keys to the mansion of a deceased aunt and told to help herself to whatever she wanted.

"What do we have?"

"There's a lot of good stuff, but some real nightmares too. More than half will have to go." George handed her a copy of the Chain Diagram he had been working on.

DESIGN		MANUFACTURING
	STRATEGIC	
	TACTICAL	
	OPERATIONAL	
	CONTINUOUS	

"There's a lot of duplication of products between the two companies," he said. "Some will have to go. So that starts us off with *Design, Strategic*."

"Good, that'll have an impact on *Design, Operational*," Elinor countered. "We'll integrate the sales force and we'll need new catalogues."

"*Manufacturing, Strategic* will pose a problem. Not only are we going to cut the product range, but we'll need to shed capacity. Get Haroldson from Luton to look at Empire's plant and equipment. Some of it might be worth taking into AEL's factories."

Elinor grimaced at the thought of shifting expensive, and often temperamental, precision machinery.

"It'll be a bit of a struggle to do this quickly," George continued. "They've had 40 years to get into this mess and we should pace ourselves. There's no point in running around like a headless chicken."

"No, George, I think we should press ahead a.s.a.p.," she said. "We've got a blueprint in front of us, the Chain Diagram, this'll see us through. In fact, I'll race you to the finish. I bet you I can finish one side of the chain sooner than you."

George let loose a childlike giggle that belied his 46 years. "Which side do you want?"

"Flip a coin? You call it. George"

The 10p coin, rotating in the air, was snatched by George and slapped on the back of his hand. "Heads!" he called out.

"Heads it is!" squealed Elinor.

"I'll take manufacturing."

"Even though I've a head-start on design?" questioned Elinor.

"Don't worry, I'll catch up. What are the ground rules."

"We work our way through the chains within a year. Ideally finding new ways of doing things at three-monthly intervals. The ideas will need to be analysed, tested and accepted as workable before you get any points. If one of us gets stuck, the other can help. The first to complete the chain, or the one with the most links, wins."

With an overdose of school boy enthusiasm, George began to fill in the Chain Diagram and starting scratching his head about how to catch up with Elinor.

DESIGN		MANUFACTURING
Cut product duplication	STRATEGIC	Cut capacity
	TACTICAL	
Integrate sales forces; new catalogues	OPERATIONAL	
	CONTINUOUS	

At the end of the first week of their race, Elinor met George to discuss progress. Deciding to cut Empire's capacity as well as its competing product range meant a swift review of the market share, revenue and profit from the plants and products about to be axed. It was proving to be an enormous task. Fortunately, most of AEL's senior management had been trained for just this type of operation, and it would just be a matter of countless late nights and busy weekends.

George looked across the board table at Elinor and spoke slowly. "It might be unreasonable to expect major break-throughs in each link, but I think simple ideas can easily lead us on elsewhere."

"I suspect you have a few ideas, George Dartry," Elinor said firmly.

Trying to muster as much subtlety as possible, he offered: "We could try something with distribution."

"I thought we were integrating that well enough."

"I was thinking of something a little more radical," George said intriguingly.

"Like what?"

George decided it was now time to reveal his hand fully. "Like getting rid of it entirely."

"What do you mean?" She pulled her chair closer to George.

"AEL has scores of trucks, drivers, back-up systems, the

whole works," he said. "And now we have Empire's to mesh together. Do we need them?"

"You mean Empire's?"

"No, I mean all of it?"

"How can we deliver our goods then?" Elinor pointedly asked.

"We contract someone else to do it. Just sell off the trucks and retrain the drivers." George now beamed a broad smile. "It can be done, it's just a matter of time before some of our competitors do it."

On the Chain Diagram wall chart now hanging in the boardroom, George inserted 'sub-contract distribution' under the *MANUFACTURING, STRATEGIC* link. George, stretching his arms behind his heads, put his feet up on the walnut table and grinned a self-satisfied smile.

By the end of the first quarter, Elinor had still not found the quantum leap that she had been was looking for. George's idea of farming out distribution was moving closer to reality, and she was still looking at the gaping holes in her Design Chain.

One morning, while waiting for her coffee to brew, she sat thoughtfully in her kitchen. As she stared into a bowl of muesli, she could hear her 18-year-old daughter Elena rummaging through her wardrobe.

"Mother! Can I borrow your Hermes scarf?" Elena called down from the landing.

"No, you may not, that's my favourite," Elinor shouted back.

Now sticking her head around the corner at the bottom of the stairs, Elena tried again. "How about your cashmere pullover – the one from Liberty's?" she said more gently.

Elinor did not allow the softer, more persuasive tone to find its mark. "When you can afford it, buy your own. Try again."

In desperation, Elena tried one final time. "Mother, you're really not helping. Okay, last chance to show you're a human being. The cream silk blouse. You know, from M&S."

Elinor relented. "Okay, but leave everything else."

As the coffee gurgled into the pot, hissed and spat a last

few drops, a thought struck Elinor. Clothes! Marks & Spencer, Liberty's, Hermes. Three different tiers, three different prices, three different markets but all superbly made. Absently, she spooned sugar and cream into her coffee and by the time Elena reappeared in the £14.95 silk blouse, Elinor looked half-frozen in thought.

"Mother are you alright? You look like you've seen a ghost."

It took Elinor as few seconds to reply. "I'm fine. I'm just thinking about armoured cars and electric motors."

"Oh, mother, give it a rest. Well, what do you think?"

"You look splendid darling," she said automatically. "It suits you. Keep it."

Elena looked stunned. "Really? You *are* a bit off this morning. Oh well, pity I didn't try on your Hardy Amies. Bye for now."

By the time Elinor arrived at the office, George was beginning to worry. She was more than an hour late and had failed to answer her home telephone. Suspecting something was amiss, he hurried down the hall to greet his sister as soon as he saw her driving into the car park.

Bustling through the corridor, pulling her coat off, and stuffing papers into a pocket, she announced to George she had solved one of the problems dogging AEL and Empire. Like a whirlwind, she gusted into the boardroom. Rhetorically she asked George, what was the common denominator between Marks & Spencer, Liberty's, and haute couture. He hesitated a moment, saying yes they all made clothes, but price might be a difference, quality was a factor.

Elinor sat at the top of the boardroom table. "Let me help. They all meet their market's expectations. If you buy at one end of the range you expect a certain price and quality, which will be different from the other end. Don't you see, our products have to meet a whole range of expectations as far apart as M&S is from Yves St Laurent. We have to structure our products and then structure our production. Understand?"

"How does it work in reality?" George sounded a bit hesitant.

"Three tiers," Elinor explained. "For instance, we could start with a standard model of armoured vehicles, with very short delivery times and few held in stock. Add to this another tier, with special options. Say a desert option and an arctic option – this can be our designer label version. Both versions are made as similar as possible, with just the different extras added on. Then we have the haute couture, one-offs requiring all our specialist skills and design abilities."

"It sounds like it could work. This is the DESIGN, TACTICS bit you've been looking for, isn't it?"

"Isn't it great! We cut inventories, speed deliveries, reduce working capital and improve our cash flow!" She almost exploded with excitement.

"Plus," George suggested, "you can charge a bit extra for the specials. You could even link the sale of standard models to a special. You know like a command vehicle directing others."

Elinor was by now overflowing with enthusiasm. "Yes, George, you've got it."

"No, Elinor, you did it, but I've got something else which might match your part of the chain." He paused for a moment. "I've been thinking about MANUFACTURING, TACTICS. What I'm about to suggest might be rocking the boat too much, but hear me out. It's the 1900."

"You mean our ICL computer?" Knowing full well how many thousands of man hours had been invested in the ICL system so far, Elinor wanted to know what was wrong with the computer.

Not wishing to usurp Elinor's position, George continued somewhat hesitantly. "Well, we've pushed it as far as we can, and we've had plenty of help from ICL. But I think it might be time to start shopping around. The IBM 4300 is what everyone's talking about and unless we do something quickly we're going to be up the river without an abacus."

Elinor wondered what was the problem. If they needed a new computer system, then they should buy one.

Knowing full well the political implications of jettisoning a British-made computer in favour of an American rival, George tried to be as diplomatic as possible. "Well, the MoD has subtle ways of putting pressure on companies like us. We could stand to lose some contracts if we bought American instead of sticking with British."

"George," Elinor retorted, "we will not endanger our competitiveness because Whitehall wants to keep jobs in Putney. Get IBM and ICL here in the same room and let them fight it out. If it's a draw, we'll follow your instincts."

The contrast between the blue-suited, white-shirted sales representatives from IBM and the regionally-accented programmers turned salesmen from ICL was noticeable.

Selection of final hardware revolved around the choice of the software package which would be used for manufacturing, planning and control. IBM presented its Communications Oriented Production and Inventory Control System, or COPICS, and ICL came with On-line Manufacturing and Control, or OMAC. George began to wonder whether anything to do with computers could be discussed without acronyms. Eventually, it became clear that the COPICS package, which had its origins in a series of theoretical works tantalisingly known as the 'Black Books', had the stronger following. So the decision was not difficult to make.

With the issue of computers temporarily out of the way, George and Elinor began looking at AEL under a microscope and, like a corporate Dr Frankenstein, set about dissecting parts of the old Empire company to graft onto their own company.

Unfortunately, much of what they found was mediocre. Some valuable senior managers who had held on by their fingertips when they discovered a takeover was possible were rescued and given new responsibilities in the enlarged AEL. Others were given help in finding new jobs.

The thorny question of computers was finally settled in IBM's favour and George, encouraged by some computer programmers from Empire, began experimenting with computer-aided design techniques which they had first introduced on a Ministry of Defence design contract.[1]

Elinor, by now obsessed with the Design function of the company, trawled through the rapidly vanishing Empire to see what could be salvaged. In some nooks were hidden long-forgotten PAM induction motors[2] and assorted engineering relics which, if they had been used wisely, might have made Empire's struggle for survival less difficult.

Standing proudly in the middle of one of the plants was a

highly-sophisticated relic from Empire's MoD work in the late 1970s. A little-used £600,000 three-dimensional milling machine which had been bought, at taxpayer's expense of course, to complete a contract to produce special bearings.

Here it was! This could be the catalyst, she thought. Elinor checked through the milling machine's preventive maintenance record.[3] It had hardly been used 100 hours over a six-month period. From the pristine condition of the machine, it still had a lot of life left in it. The idiots, they never looked beyond what they were supposed to produce, she mused, but this machine had the potential to manufacture something really special.

She telephoned George for a second opinion. Yes, he remembered the three-dimensional milling machine, and what a waste it had seemed. Yes, it could be operational quite quickly. Of course, the design director could look at it. No, there was little need to shift the machine since he had arranged a regular despatch service between the company's network of four plants.

"Come on, Elly, you're teasing me, what do you have?"

"Well, George, we revolutionised washing machines in the 1970s, and we're going to do it again in the 1980s."

"How?"

"With this machine, Empire made some of the best bearings in the world. We still make the best motors. Hey, presto. A new washing machine."

George felt he had missed the point. "I might sound a bit dim, but I don't follow."

"Every washing machine uses a long fan belt to turn the drum," she began to explain slowly. "With a special bearing, we can have a direct drive model. Of course, it will put enormous forces on the motor, but we can handle that if we can make a new bearing with this milling machine. A stronger bearing will take the strain. It's magic. Fewer parts, cheaper assembly and easier maintenance. I think you'd better add this to the Chain Diagram."

From the time of the takeover of Empire in October 1981, AEL had undergone a transformation itself. It had streamlined its product range, restructured its design approach to existing products and integrated two sets of sales teams. Furthermore, three Empire factories had been closed and distribution for the entire company had been farmed out. Finally, the new computer system was being installed.

The breathtaking pace of these changes would have left many other companies reeling with distraction. Instead, Elinor and George held regular 'milestone' meetings which focused on specific goals.[4] At one such meeting later in the year, as British unemployment threatened to reach three million for the first time since the 1930s, the two Dartrys examined even bolder ideas for improving the efficiency of the company. George now proposed that Systems Management techniques[5], already in use in the US, could be implemented in AEL. When these were added to work breakdown structures,[6] the DESIGN, TACTICAL function in the Chain Diagram could be revolutionised. And there were other ideas of using robots and avoiding bottlenecks[7] that could be applied to the MANUFACTURING, OPERATIONAL.

"I've already mentioned the robots to some of the plant managers and they've second-guessed the union reaction," George told his sister.

"What's that?"

George tittered a little. "They want to know if the robots will pay union dues."

"My God," Elinor gasped, "old habits die hard. Robots sound fine, if a bit expensive, George. But I might be able to help you with MANUFACTURING, OPERATIONAL if you like."

George nodded in agreement, wondering what his sister could have come up with.

"How efficient do you think we are?" she asked.

George smiled to himself as he recalled asking the AEL board the same question almost 10 years earlier. "Almost impossible to tell," he admitted.

"Put it another way, what benchmark do we have for judging our performance?"

"Profit, earnings per share, and share price are the usual measures."

"No, I mean within the plants. You know like units made, set-up times."

George now saw what Elinor was getting at. "You're talking about these reports from Japan, aren't you? I don't know if they're true. How can you cut a set-up time from a couple of hours to a few minutes. It's too incredible to believe."

"But George, if it's true, we'll be looking at lowering batch sizes and increasing our order response. Think of what this could do to our working capital and our stores. And look at the chain. We haven't done anything yet about our MANUFACTURING, OPERATIONAL. There's scope in the chain for something radical like this. And don't forget what you keep saying about our competitors doing it first."

"As usual Elinor, you're right."

DESIGN		MANUFACTURING
Cut product duplication; launch new product line	STRATEGIC	Cut capacity; sub-contract distribution
Three-tier product range	TACTICAL	New IBM computer system
Integrate sales forces; new catalogues	OPERATIONAL	Robotics; quick set-ups
	CONTINUOUS	

Following this discussion on Japanese manufacturing techniques, George set in motion a series of events that would eventually lead AEL into the vanguard of British engineering excellence.

By the end of the week, the first step had been taken and George found himself in Tokyo. As the invited guest of Akio Rosenbaum – the closest thing to a cultural contradiction that Japan and Germany had yet created – George was left in no doubt about the future trends of the engineering industry worldwide.

Rosenbaum, who had met George at a reception in the spring and had invited him to Japan, was a few years older than his English guest, but light years ahead in understanding the mercurial mix of mind and machine that constituted brilliant engineering. He was emphatic that George would be shown everything which was transforming Japan into a technological giant. And then he would be shown how the European mind – well, German, at least – could adopt Japanese manufacturing philosophies such as Total Quality[8] and transplant them to occidental soil. Within three weeks, Rosenbaum claimed, AEL could become a World Class company.[9]

George began to liken his Japanese-German host to an intergalactic version of the legendary James Fairfax. Genial, buckets of bravado, enormous appetite and a willingness to travel and learn foreign ways.

When it came to the much-heralded quick set-ups, which George assumed would be easy to comprehend, Rosenbaum coached his guest about the frame of mind that allows the right approach to productive thinking. George viewed the philosophical packaging of the theory a little tiresome and hoped it could be dispensed with rapidly once he got back home. For the moment, like a Doubting Thomas, George challenged his host to see the reality. Show me, he said. And Rosenbaum did.

Rosenbaum had picked a simple stamping press change-over in the nearby Matsu car plant which would have taken three hours in a Manchester or Stuttgart factory. Sixteen minutes at Matsu. "Don't blink," joked Rosenbaum in a slight American accent, "or you might miss it!"

A further demonstration at a forging plant saw a standard two-hour European set-up for making push rods routinely carried out in three minutes.

Humbled and converted, George waited for further mysteries to be unfolded. And Rosenbaum did not fail him.

Meanwhile back in England, Elinor was struggling with how to finish off the Design Chain. She suspected that George would return with a strong enough grasp of the quick set-up approach that they would be neck and neck in their race to the finish.

She began to berate herself for not being able to find a new DESIGN, CONTINUOUS phase of the chain. This part of the chain had been her own idea, and while she knew in her heart that the logic and theory were correct, she couldn't find a realistic instance of how constantly to improve the design function within the company. She looked for examples in food retailing, aviation, shipbuilding, car manufacturing, even in financial services. Yet nothing seemed to give her a lead.

Jogging through the open country west of Mansfield one morning with her daughter, she asked herself countless questions. How do we give the customer the best part of the design chain? How do we guarantee that we're giving them what they want – continuously. She saw Elena running ahead and thought how she had stumbled across a new idea just by listening to her daughter. But, lightning doesn't strike twice, she thought. I'm on my own.

She thought of the wad of faxes George had sent to her the night before. He seemed to be having the time of his life, especially with some German chap. She could always give George a call and try to talk things through with him, but resisted the temptation. No, she insisted, she would see this through by herself. She wouldn't run asking for help. Her customers didn't do it and she wasn't about to do it either. Then she thought, that's it!

She began breathing harder going up the hill past Mercer Pond but a gentle breeze cooled her. Why did a customer not run to a manufacturer to consult him about parts of a design? Perhaps because no one would take him seriously. Or the manufacturer might not respond to the customer's requests.

But what if a manufacturer could respond more quickly to specific design requests? This could link him more closely with the customer. It could be a way of locking in customers, of making them dependent on the manufacturer for future products and in turn guaranteeing the manufacturer future markets. It would be a real case of chaining the customer to the manufacturer. What beautiful irony! Chains!

Now heading downhill, with Elena a good half mile ahead of her, Elinor quickened her mental pace. She began thinking how a team of AEL designers could be created to start the design process in the customer's own offices. Four, maybe five, talented designers could be rotated through their major clients, spending weeks on big projects and half-days when nothing much was happening.

The more she thought about it, the more she liked it. Plant the designers in the customer's premises and watch them grow! She was so enthusiastic with the idea that on impulse she detoured from her normal route home, and jogged an extra two miles to the AEL factory in Mansfield. With a crimson face and aching legs, she sprinted in past the front desk, just briefly waving to the receptionist. Down the corridor, into the telex room where she found the fax machine. She scribbled a message on a sheet of paper, dialled George's hotel in Tokyo and faxed the words: *FOUND IT*.

A sense of smug satisfaction engulfed her for the rest of the day. She had showered and changed in the office and was about to go for lunch when her secretary stopped her in her tracks. It was a message from George: *ME TOO!*

Three days later, a red-eyed George sat in Elinor's kitchen, listening to his sister and niece having a heated discussion upstairs over clothes and boyfriends. The coffee machine gurgled and the smell of warm croissants pervaded the air. When Elinor reappeared she was shaking her head in annoyance. "Teenagers!"

But she quickly outlined her *DESIGN, CONTINUOUS* idea to George who immediately saw the tremendous potential of her roving design team. Then it was George's turn.

"Elly, I went looking for *MANUFACTURING, OPERATIONAL* but also found *MANUFACTURING, CONTINUOUS*. I found a whole ethos of manufacturing that's alien to us. They have thousands of robots,[10] something called quality circles, an unbelievable thing called Just-in-Time[11] and some great ideas on plant loading.[12] We're going to be submerged by Japanese design and products sooner than anyone imagined."

Elinor filled his cup with fresh coffee.

"The Just-in-Time idea is simplicity itself," he continued. "You only stock enough components for a day's production instead of a week. You virtually cut out the stock room and pass the responsibility back to the supplier. Suddenly, it's his job to get the components to you just in time when you need them.

"George, that's brilliant!" Elinor erupted.

"I think our chain race is a photo-finish, a draw," he said mildly.

"Yes, I'll settle for a draw."

DESIGN		MANUFACTURING
Cut product duplication; launch new product line	*STRATEGIC*	Cut capacity; sub-contract distribution
Three-tier product range	*TACTICAL*	New IBM computer system
Integrate sales forces; new catalogues	*OPERATIONAL*	Robotics; quick set-ups
Customer-based design teams	*CONTINUOUS*	Just-in-Time

"Although, I do have one final suggestion," George added. "It could be strategic, perhaps tactical."

"What are you thinking about now?" asked Elinor.

"Well, I told you about Rosenbaum. I suggested to him that we swap half of our North Sea stake for one of his distribution companies in Germany. If we can get a toe-hold in Germany we'll be strategically placed for years ahead. They're our toughest competitors but I think we can beat them on their own turf with Japanese engineering techniques and British labour."

Elinor frowned at the thought of surrendering valuable North Sea oil revenues.

"Don't worry about the oil, Elly. It was an enabler, never a success factor[13] – just a means to an end."

Elinor felt pain at the thought of losing something that had cost so much in family terms, namely the death of her brother James. But George persisted. "We got Empire because of it," he argued, "but the age of cheap oil is here again. We've got to look to the future."

"Maybe you're right. But who'll run the German side of things?"

"I was coming to that bit. We'll need someone with a fresh perspective to the chains and ..."

George's flow was interrupted by a crashing, thumping sound coming down the staircase. Then, standing in the kitchen doorway, was Elena, wearing her mother's Gloria Vanderbilt jeans and her own faded 'Atomkraft? Nein Danke' T-shirt.

"Hi, uncle George, god you look dreadful," she said.

"Thanks, Elena, I needed that."

Ignoring her daughter, Elinor tried to resume the conversation. "You were saying something about fresh perspectives for Germany?"

"Yes, well," George fumbled and looking a little sheepishly he gestured to Elena. "You're looking at her!"

Turning to look at her daughter, Elinor's jaw dropped in disbelief. "You cannot be serious!"

Chapter Notes

The harsh economic conditions in Britain during the early 1980s dealt a severe blow to many small industrial companies as high interest rates, diminishing markets and a strong pound fostered cutthroat competition. And despite enormous political goodwill, thousands of small companies went bankrupt. Britain, more than ever, became a country of large corporations.

The Conservative government insisted, like Edward Heath had done nine years earlier, that private industry had to stand on its own feet. It was clear, however, that private capital, left to its own devices, would not provide the huge investments required for new risky technologies.

A succession of institutions and specially-established bodies tried to bring government and industry closer together. Politicians and voters, however, found it easier to turn away from the unsavoury problems of industrial decline. Instead, privatisation and the 'free market' were seen as solutions to industry's malaise.

Reference Notes

[1]For AEL, it was ironic that something as sophisticated as computer-aided design, the use of computer-based techniques to aid design engineering draughting activities, should emanate from a company in such dire financial straits as Empire Engineering. None the less, given that AEL now had a corporate culture that openly encouraged revolutionary approaches to engineering, swift progress was possible.

CAD systems were born in the early 1970s with the first system suppliers who took advantage of developing technologies such as interactive processing, graphics display terminals and the mathematics for representing product geometrics. The cost of these early systems was high and generally limited to aerospace and automotive companies. By the late 1970s, CAD became more widely accepted with the improved price/performance of computers. The early 1980s saw further technological advances with the introduction of intelligent workstations and master display screens.

The distinguishing feature of any CAD system is the display terminal which shows a graphical representation of a part or an assembly. Using a variety of input devices, a designer creates a design for a part, an assembly, an electronic schematic or layout, complete with dimensions and notes. The workstation or terminal displays a graphical representation of the design that interactively reflects the changes the designer makes.

A CAD system creates a geometric model of the design which is stored in a database. Once a design is created it is not necessary to re-draw it as it can be recalled from the database and re-used. Thus the model is retained and modified for re-use in similar designs.

By the mid-1980s, CAD technology had made a number of important strides forward such as the development of Engineering Data Management Systems (EDMS) which provided some automated control and access to the large CAD-generated databases of geometric data. Normal database retrieval programs were unable to cope with the applications programming needed to control the technical aspects of engineering change control and configuration control.

The need of customers to have control over the design documentation of their suppliers also increased. The US Department of Defense pushed this further and introduced Computer Aided Logistics System (CALS) which aimed to standardise the interfaces to defence suppliers' EDMSs.

[2]By the 1950s, it seemed that technical development of the electric motor was complete, but in 1957 Professor G. H. Rawcliffe developed the pole amplitude modulated, or PAM, motor. This is an inductive motor whose field coils are so arranged that by interchanging a few connections the number of poles can be changed. Since the speed of an AC motor is determined by the number of poles (as well as the supply frequency), this gave a motor which could be switched between two distinct values. A PAM induction

motor, therefore, retains the reliability and robustness of the conventional induction motor but can work at different speeds.

PAM motors have now been largely replaced with power semi-conductors which change the supply frequency and produce true variable speed control. By the early 1970s, even the largest motors could be controlled by semi-conductor frequency convertors.

[3]Within any large modern engineering works, preventive maintenance, or the periodic checking of equipment, plant, building and machines, is an important technique for discovering potential problems that could lead to equipment breakdown or early depreciation. Preventive maintenance requires careful scheduling of the maintenance crews and equipment if production delays are not to occur. It thus can only be used effectively when a computer-aided system is installed.

[4]By using 'milestone' meetings as checkpoints through this race to complete the chain, Elinor and George were able to ensure that the project was on course and accurately moving towards its final objective.

Project management techniques which focus on the achievement of milestones rather than completion of activities evolved from the oil industry and defence equipment manufacturers. The advantage of goal-directed milestone planning is that fewer milestones are needed than activities and that the project teams are more able to be creative about the solutions.

[5]Introduced by Boeing in the 1970s, Systems Management techniques for project management are a highly structured framework within which a development project is planned and executed. Each phase is terminated by the preparation and authorisation of design documentation by the project manager. Each phase must be completed before the next can begin.

[6]AEL's use of work breakdown structures would enable it to plan large development projects. As a technique, the approach assumes the functions of each part of a complex product are independent of each other or that the interface between functions can be carefully specified. In this way, different teams can be set up to develop each module in the work breakdown structure. This approach is often

used in automotive and aerospace development to avoid unwieldy teams.

[7]In the early 1980s, the concept of scheduling only the 'bottleneck' machines in a plant and allowing others to work when they had spare capacity and available work was developed by Eliyahu Goldratt. Central to this idea was the construction of a computer program called OPT (Optimised Technology). Goldratt spelled out the problems of bottlenecks in production and outlined the theory behind solving them in *The Goal* (Gower, 1984).

[8]Whereas George had already concluded that the manufacture of quality products was a key method of reducing waste (the operational component of his Manufacturing Chain), he was now shown a far more comprehensive approach to quality, namely Total Quality, which pervaded entire organisations.

The Total Quality technique entails the integration of the continuous quality improvement efforts of people at all levels in the organisation to deliver products and services which ensure customer satisfaction.

Although Total Quality has its roots in the post-war economic renaissance of Japan, Western interest in the philosophy blossomed only during the 1980s in the face of repeatedly successful Japanese corporate assaults on US and European markets. At long last, the founding fathers of total quality – Deming, Duran and Crosby – were given the recognition they deserved by Western management. By now displaying all the vigour of a convert, many occidental companies started to set quality standards that would have been considered unattainable years earlier – such as Motorola's rejection target of less than one part per 10 million.

In the event, the bulk of best practice in Total Quality thinking began to emanate from the US and Britain, with the Western approach emphasising 'business purpose' and 'continuous improvement'.

[9]Throughout the 1980s, manufacturing businesses looked internationally for examples of operations they could copy to improve their own performance – JIT, Total Quality, Time Based Management, etc. The idea began to emerge that by benchmarking competitors and operations in different sectors to create World Class (from 'best in class') standards, targets could be set for individual improvement in

performance. These ideas were developed by Richard Schonberg in his book *World Class Manufacturing*.

[10]Rapid development of microprocessors during the 1980s, when combined with the use of reliable electromechanical mechanisms, set the stage for a phenomenal increase in the world population of robots. As a manufacturing tool, robots work best in conditions where the production process has been simplified to basic movements and decision-making, thereby permitting the use of unskilled labour.

The word 'robot' comes from the Czech for 'forced labour' and was first used as a term for a mechanical contrivance with human attributes by Karel Capek (1890-1938) in his 1920 play *R.U.R.* (Rossum's Universal Robots). Capek's leading character Rossum asserts that a human being is someone who likes to feel happy, go for a walk, or perhaps even do something entirely pointless. In stark contrast, robots are by definition not expected to display any such human characteristics but instead are obliged to perform only those functions which expedite the task at hand.

[11]Rosenbaum may have been the first to show George a Just-in-Time system in operation, but the Englishman's familiarity with car manufacturing in Britain would already have given him an insight into some of the principles behind the philosophy.

In fact, many of the fundamentals behind Just-in-Time have been apparent in Western manufacturing since the 1920s, during which period the Ford Motor Company reduced its production cycle from 21 to 14 days. However, because Western countries generally have abundant space, energy and material resources, high-performing manufacturing companies learned to cultivate customer demand for change and variety. Turning out new products and holding large volumes of goods in inventory in order to respond to customer demand were two of the main aims of a company. As for 'waste' in the form of potentially defective parts and the misuse of large amounts of capital tied-up in inventory, these were not dominant concerns.

[12]Acceptance of the JIT philosophy led George down several avenues that would make a significant contribution to AEL's manufacturing potential. One such concept was Uniform Plant Load

(UPL) which is based on the simple precept that if you sell daily, then make it daily. This means that every part is manufactured in small lots on a daily basis. Wherever possible (and it is almost always possible) each item is manufactured to demand not to stock. However, in order to achieve this, most companies are required to reduce dramatically their manufacturing lead times.

[13]AEL's North Sea stake, although it provided financial insulation during the early 1980s recession, never distracted the company from its primary activity of an engineering company. In this regard, AEL was conscious that its Critical Success Factors, or the things it needed to do well in order to achieve its strategic goals, were in the engineering industry. Originally suggested by D. Rokaert in the US to link information strategy studies to the business goals of the enterprise, 'critical success factors' as a term has now entered common business usage.

Chapter Fourteen – 1982

De Lorean Motors in receivership; Israel invades Lebanon;
"ET"; "The Eye of the Tiger"

No, it wasn't a belated April Fool's Day joke as some had hoped. It was a major international incident which seemed to be escalating out of control.

George tuned into the World Service for further news. It was April 2, 1982, and Argentina had just invaded the Falklands Islands.

Now in something of a tizz, he tried telephoning Elinor again but there was no reply. Damn it, he thought, where do these women get to?

There was a knock on the front door. It was Elinor. She had heard the news on the radio and came straight to George's house.

Both Dartrys had one thing in mind and there was very little preamble to their discussion, which focused on a new vehicle prototype that they had been talking over in recent weeks. No drawings for the vehicle existed, no plans had been drawn up, it was simply a hypothetical construct at the moment. Without really being sure if the vehicle could be made, they were now trying to decide whether to put the idea to the Ministry of Defence anyway.

It was so revolutionary, George contended, that they might damage their reputations by telling Ministry officials too early. But Elinor was right, he acknowledged, when she said they had to make the maximum effort in this time of national emergency. Torn between these conflicting emotions, they did the most sensible thing in the circumstances, which was to ignore the problem of the Ministry for the moment and see if some progress could be made elsewhere.

Not much work was needed on the theory of this new vehicle, which was elementary enough. It all hinged on replacing the traditional armour of an armoured car with a lighter stronger material. In layman's terms, it was akin to the polyfibre material used to make bullet proof vests but produced in a different fashion.

The real progress needed now was in the processing technology – namely, how to make the polyfibres into panels large enough to replace sheet metal. And the one thing that was holding them back from instituting immediate trials was AEL's new computer system, which despite having been introduced several months earlier, was proving to be a real nightmare. Neither Elinor nor George were entirely convinced that the system was sufficiently operational and reliable help them to solve the problems they now faced.

"We do have a little time on our side," George concluded. "If the islands are to be recaptured, it'll take weeks to get enough men down there."

Elinor asked how long he thought it would be before British troops landed in the Falklands.

"Two, maybe, three weeks," he said thoughtfully.

This brief 'window of opportunity' did not leave much room for miscalculation and, since the IBM 4300 had been installed, errors had been unearthed every few hours.

As computers go, the 4300 was a masterpiece of electronic engineering. It represented such amazing future potential that once the decision had been taken to abandon the old ICL workhorse, AEL took the plunge in a big way. A new air-conditioned computer room was built and the existing computer department staff was more than doubled. Although AEL's huge investment amounted to an initial outlay of £250,000 with annual running costs well in excess of £300,000, there was an intense belief that the computer system would revolutionise the entire company. A new era of swift and constant change would accompany the 4300, first in the production of bills of material and stock control, and later in purchasing, shop orders, forecasting and ultimately cost accounting.

However, this utopian future, so clear in the minds of IBM representatives and AEL senior staff, was now faltering at the first obstacle. In fact, absurdly complicated computer procedures were dictating wholesale changes in the way AEL carried on its business. Even the most basic items in the creation of a product, such as bills of material, were turned upside down following attempts to get the company's entire parts list into the computer. Given that AEL's existing parts list was based on design features – namely, technical functions rather than methods of assembly – this was no easy task. Early estimates suggested that it would take two years to change the 100,000 part numbers, an undertaking not eased by the fact that some part numbers were not unique, and that the final digit of many 12-digit numbers was missing. The prodigious nature of the task was complicated even further by the recent absorption of many identical parts from Empire Engineering.

Computerisation would ultimately chart a way out of this quagmire by abolishing part numbers entirely and replacing them with codes which could be called up on a video display unit to indicate every design and production feature of the part concerned. But for the moment, computerisation was the source of the problem and the tetchy shop floor of AEL was in chaos.

Hoping to overcome the maze of complexity generated by computerisation, Elinor now suggested the creation of a special Product Group[1] and a set of unique part numbers for the new experimental vehicle. These numbers might only be necessary for a couple of weeks, after which they could be wiped from the computer if necessary. And in the meantime, they could be used to expedite materials from work in progress in other parts of the AEL group.

While Elinor and George were determining whether their as yet untested theory was sound, the design department began to sketch out rough ideas for their radically different vehicle. Central to the design would be a weight saving of about a ton. Suddenly a whole range of options appeared, such as increasing the speed and range of an existing armoured personnel carrier by fitting a new engine and auxiliary fuel tanks, and extending the wheel base to carry 15 men instead of the standard nine.

Elinor reminded George that what they had in effect was a miniature chain in operation, one which had begun with the strategic decision to pursue the polyfibre. And already some other factors such as tactics and operational considerations were coming into play. As for theory, the early signs were that sufficient polyfibre could be 'welded' into panels large enough for personnel carriers. Overseeing the design chain was Bill Finston, who now requested assistance from some old friends at a Formula One racing team in Woking.

"Formula One?" a perplexed George quizzed him. "We are talking about the same project, aren't we?"

Accustomed to dealing with obscure solutions to arcane problems, Finston explained that modern racing car designers were now using so many new materials and construction techniques that they could prove crucial in their own prototype. A racing car, Finston added, was a harmonious design of speed, strength and safety. All he had to do was make one that was bulletproof as well.

George, in the meantime, had located several dozen polyfibre panels, enough to start their experiments. The edges of these 12in x 18in pieces were carefully opened and once the fibres were teased out to look like little tufts of carpet, they were 'welded' together with a hastily-assembled laser that had been borrowed by Finston from the physics lab of Southampton University. Slowly, almost tuft by tuft, the panels were meshed together until Finston had formed a 6ft x 3ft panel. Now large enough to replicate the side of a personnel carrier, the polyfibre panel was fixed to a hefty tubular steel frame.

An attempt to set up a firing range within the grounds of AEL proved well nigh impossible without cordoning off half the factory. George briefly thought about night testing before finally agreeing to telephone the Manchester police training authority. Somewhat sceptical at first, the police authority realised how serious George was when he pulled up into their car park with the large polyfibre panel sitting in the back seat of the Napier alongside Finston.

Two trained marksmen had been seconded for the duration of the trial, which over the course of several hours saw them test an assortment of weapons with ear-splitting results.

"Keep firing at the black joints," George urged them, "hit the joints first." George and Finston had assumed that the weakest part of the polyfibre panels would be their crude laser 'welds'. Volley after volley was fired into them but with little or no penetration on the inside of the polyfibre panel. The joints, if anything, appeared to be stronger than the rest of the panel.

Effective against snipers, thought George, but what about something stronger? Thanking the Manchester constabulary for their assistance, he returned with the slightly battered fibre panel to the AEL works.

As a result of the police tests, George and Finston began thinking about fresh experiments, some of which would involve 'baking' the panels with the laser. If the original 'welds' had actually strengthened the polyfibre, they now hypothesised that whatever chemical or physical change had occurred should be extended to the entire fibre panel, in effect cooking or 'baking' it harder.

By Tuesday afternoon, the day after the British task force set sail from Portsmouth and Lord Carrington resigned as Foreign Secretary, Elinor was ready to make contact with the MoD. Work was already underway on converting a pair of personnel carriers, prepared with 'baked' and 'unbaked' fibre panels, for testing on the Salisbury Plain. All that would be needed now was the go-ahead from Whitehall.

But in their own excitement, Elinor and George had ignored the near panic that had engulfed the British government. In the pandemonium, an entire class of cool-headed career civil servants had suddenly become energised to the point of hyperactivity. Each was chasing progress on a dozen issues and promised Elinor they would return her telephone call. None did. "They're more interested chasing knighthoods than in testing our vehicles," quipped Elinor.

But then geography, and the 8,000 mile voyage to the Falklands, came to the rescue.

By the end of the first week, most of the Whitehall departments had committed themselves to immediate action. Hectic preparations had been made in an uncharacteristically rushed manner. Now with the Task Force on the high seas, there was time for these career civil servants to sit back and reflect on their work. And, all of a sudden, with time on their hands, doubts began to creep into their normally conservative minds. Had they done enough? Could more have been done? Was there anything left undone?

By noon on Friday, Elinor took her third telephone call from those elusive mandarins asking what exactly did she want to do.

Testing, they promised, could take place on Monday. No, she insisted, it had to be Saturday. Without much further discussion, they relented. All of a sudden, that which had been impossible to achieve just days earlier was swiftly rubber-stamped. A Ministry of Defence firing range near the Salisbury Plain was earmarked for AEL on Saturday morning. If additional tests were necessary, the Whitehall civil servants now obligingly offered, these could be continued on Monday.

Meanwhile in the Mansfield factory, George and Bill Finston had already dissected two personnel carriers in the hope of securing the permission for the firing range. These two vehicles had huge 3ft squares cut out of their sides. Further square holes were cut from the vehicles' top and back. And bolted over these openings were large polyfibre panels on tubular frames. One vehicle was fitted with the normal untreated polyfibre while a second was protected with the baked version of the panels.

With a three-hour testing session allocated to AEL, the plan was to fire four missiles at half-hourly intervals at the targets. It was hoped that the personnel carriers would survive one, possibly two, hits but certainly no more than that. With a number of video recorders set up at pre-determined vantage points, this total destructive testing would hopefully reveal all they needed to know.

On schedule, precisely at 10.10 am on Saturday morning, Elinor, George and a Captain Porter watched from a dugout as the first ground-to-ground missile was fired. A split second later, a ball of flame erupted and the deafening explosion shook the dugout.

Scanning the debris as the smoke cleared, Elinor wondered what, if anything, could have survived the explosion. On closer inspection of the scorched polyfibre panels, a large hole the size of a football was clearly visible at the point of impact. George and Elinor surveyed the blackened interior of the vehicle and first impressions were not too optimistic.

Captain Porter, their minder for the morning testing, seemed to be more impressed with the wrecked vehicle than they were. "Interesting," he muttered, "not bad."

Thirty minutes later, the second missile was fired into the other side of the same target. This explosion ripped through the vehicle, buckling the sheet metal roof and punching out the rear doors.

The three ear-muffed spectators slowly made their way to the wreckage and in silence surveyed the extent of the damage. It was a total wreck, with loose scorched polyfibre panels dangling on the heavy tubular frames. A complete write-off. All hopes were now placed on the third and fourth firings.

For the next firing, again on schedule at 11.10 am, George had arranged this time for the second personnel carrier to be protected with the 'baked' panels. Again they watched in silence as a fireball engulfed the vehicle a split second after impact. And this time, instead of finding a football-sized hole in the polyfibre panel, they found a smaller hole, perhaps the size of a tennis ball.

"Now, we're getting somewhere," said Captain Porter.

Half an hour later, as they picked their way through an assortment of tail fins and engine housings after the fourth and final missile had been fired, George and Elinor felt their instincts were proving correct. The last explosion had pushed the polyfibre panel in considerably, but when the rear doors were opened, the interior of the vehicle was largely intact, with the exception of one hole. The polyfibre panels had dissipated the impact of two direct hits. When Finston started the engine in the vehicle without difficulty, there were broad smiles of satisfaction.

Elinor now triggered their plan of action. While she dashed back to the Albion works, George, in his customary fashion, would deal with the MoD administrators. And Finston was left in charge of picking up the pieces of the target vehicles for return to Mansfield. They were now about to embark on the next stage of their chain.

Using some technical guidance from the Woking racing car designers, Finston had finally settled on a combination of space frame and monocoque construction, the two traditional methods of building high performance racing cars.

But almost as soon as the design had been settled, problems developed on the Mansfield shop floor. Elinor's special numbering system for the Falklands vehicle ran into immediate problems with wrong parts being delivered to the assembly line. In one case where two ounces of oil were requested, the computer authorised delivery of two gallons of diesel fuel to the line. Tubular framing, more suited for garden furniture, turned up instead of the heavy-gauge tubing that Finston needed. Inexplicably, several double-glazed office windows were delivered to the assembly area, followed by boxes of office stationery and coloured pencils. Finston noted wryly such things might help everyone pass the time but were doing little to build an armoured vehicle. In fact, the IBM computer, already discredited in the eyes of many on the shopfloor, was being fed inadequate information and, not surprisingly, mistakes were cropping up everywhere along the production line.

And AEL's traditionally unruffled workforce began to find the sudden appearance of this completely new vehicle in their factory too much to cope with. Suddenly a serious industrial relations problem was in the making until George pleaded at a mass meeting for everyone to pull together in this time of national emergency.

Considering himself a well-versed armchair military strategist, George had concluded that the British supply lines were stretched so far south that the Task Force would have only one shot at retaking the Falklands. This would not be a long-drawn out affair. It would be a simple matter of victory or defeat. From this analysis, he now told the Mansfield workers that it would be all over within a couple of weeks. "Bear with me," he pleaded, "win or lose, we'll be back to normal by the end of the month."

This promise of an early return to normal working did the trick and the flicker of rebellion was effectively snuffed out.

George later likened the atmosphere in the factory to that of a deaf orchestra, conducted by a blind man. The physical energy and skills existed, as did the determination of those gathered. But before any sound could come out of the pit, everyone had to learn new ways of communicating to get over their handicaps.

And at the same time, Elinor kept reminding them that time was running out. Prototype personnel carriers would have to be assembled quickly and tested in the nearby car park. If they were lucky they would be able to airlift the first dozen to Ascension where they could be loaded onto supply ships for the final journey south.

As for the final configuration of the new 'Falklands class' vehicles, George decided it would be foolhardy to offer the MoD endless permutations on how to make use of the lighter weight of the vehicle. Instead he took matters into his own hands, and using the estimated one-ton weight saving, had extra fuel tanks fitted to the personnel carriers.

By the end of the second week after the Argentine invasion of the islands, the first dozen lightweight long-range personnel carriers were ready to go to the South Atlantic. As planned, these were airlifted to the mid-Atlantic island of Ascension where they were loaded onto a small supply ship. As this vessel joined the Task Force, an extra shift was introduced at the AEL factory to produce the next batch of vehicles.

In the coming weeks, as the military build-up continued, the vulnerability of the British supply lines to the Argentine Air Force was underscored with the sinking, on May 4, of the destroyer *Sheffield*.

Seven weeks after the invasion of the islands the Royal Marines made their successful landing at San Carlos Bay and established their positions against counter-attack. But within days of this landing, disaster struck.

During shipment, the first batch of new personnel carriers had been transferred to the container ship *Atlantic Conveyor*, which was now attacked by Argentine jets. Mistaking the supply ship for an aircraft carrier, the jets successfully fired two Exocet missiles into the vessel with devastating effect.

As the air and sea battle developed around the islands, Elinor attempted to get the second batch of personnel carriers, by now sitting on the dockside in Ascension, into the combat zone. Further British naval losses quickly followed, however, and the prototype vehicles were shunted to one side to make way for emergency deployment of additional missile batteries.

By the first week in June the panic fortunately had subsided yet again and, as the British ground forces closed in on Port Stanley, the AEL prototypes were in transit again. Ironically, the cargo ship transporting them arrived within sight of the islands on June 14, the day the Argentine commander surrendered to a Spanish-speaking British officer.

Chapter Fourteen

Although the new vehicles, which Elinor had by now christened the F-100, never actually saw action in the Falklands campaign, their development had impressed the MoD sufficiently for it to place several small orders with AEL. As for its reputation of being able to innovate under pressure, AEL had come through the Falklands conflict with flying colours.

With such promising signals as this, AEL now seemed destined to be a world class engineering company, capable of selling its products anywhere and beating any international competition. But for the rest of the decade, the reality would be different!

Reference Notes

[1]In fact, Elinor was employing a widely accepted manufacturing concept which stemmed from William Schumacher's idea that 'small is beautiful'. The principle behind Product Groups meant that manufacturing companies were organised into sub-units which performed all the operations of a fully-fledged commercial operation in that they had all the plant, men and materials necessary for operating under one manager. The Product Groups were expected to operate as small businesses within the overall company.

Historically, the concept had already been tried within the Albion company during the 1930s when Fred Carey had briefly experimented with a factory-within-a-factory for the exclusive production of motors for the Air Ministry. As military output began to dominate Albion production, this subdivision of the factory was no longer deemed feasible.

Chapter Fifteen – 1991

Break-up of the Soviet Union; Robert Maxwell dies at sea;
Terry Waite freed; "A Year in Provence"

Elinor Dartry had seemed poised on the threshold of great-
ness in the aftermath of the Falklands campaign in 1982. But
things turned out quite different than anyone imagined.

In fact, in the year of Margaret Thatcher's re-election as
prime minister, a sea change seemed to overpower Britain as a
new spirit of commercialism pulsed through the economy. A
burgeoning stock market, underpinned by a bloated financial
services industry, became the touchstone by which everything
was measured. And phrases like 'Big Bang' and 'leveraged
buyout' entered the vocabulary of the country's university
graduates.

Given that manufacturing industry was never highly
regarded in Britain anyway, the lure of the bright lights of the
City of London proved sufficient for the steady stream of
engineering graduates into British industry to be reduced to a
trickle. As university graduates turned their back on engineering during the decade, AEL, along with the rest of the
country's industrial enterprises, found itself unable to match
the enormous 'remuneration packages' on offer in the City.
There were simply not enough young engineer recruits left in
Britain.

In Elinor's view, the engineering industry had long suffered
an image problem, one that probably went back as far as the
early nineteenth century. Ask anyone what was William
Morris' claim to fame, she would moan, and the chances were
they would say he was in the Arts and Crafts movement. No
one, she complained, seemed to care about the other William
Morris who revolutionised Britain's automotive industry. And
now engineering per se simply did not appeal to young people
compared with something as new and clever as 'financial engineering.' From her standpoint, AEL and the rest of the British
industry needed to enhance the reputation of engineering as a

career. It had to be made exciting, even exotic, dynamic and highly paid. As she began grooming her daughter Elena for a future role in the company, Elinor always stressed the imaginative dimension of engineering.

But apart from indoctrinating her own daughter, Elinor, looking at the wreckage of the recession of the early 1980s, knew that large-scale remedies could not be found in Britain. She would need to look elsewhere for opportunities that would fire the imagination of young people.

In looking abroad, she searched for the most lucrative engineering markets, those where engineering skills were respected and rewarded. In the event, her gaze settled on the Middle East.

Oddly enough, AEL had never benefited much from the surge of petrodollars that flooded into the British economy during the 1970s, but Elinor was determined now to tap into this valuable source of capital. High-level meetings with Iraqui, Saudi and Syrian officials in London convinced her that there was a market in the region for some AEL military and even household products. To this end, she despatched her brother George as a plenipotentiary on an extensive tour of the Middle East.

Once in the region, George was approached at various intervals by arms dealers who were supplying each side in the Iran-Iraq military stalemate that had started in 1982. It being long-established AEL policy not to supply countries actively engaged in a military campaign, with the notable exception of Britain, George politely declined their entreaties. None the less, he suggested that when the conflict was over, they might be able to look at things again.

And this is precisely what happened within weeks of Iraqi acceptance of UN ceasefire proposals in August 1988. George was approached by Iraqi government representatives hoping to rebuild their depleted military capability. Now in the aftermath of this six-year war, many western companies, often backed by cheap government export credits, hoped to profit from the reconstruction of the shattered economies in Iran and Iraq. And AEL, still waiting for a sales breakthrough in the region, began to take the Iraqi enquiries seriously.

As a matter of routine precaution, George sent copies of his

Middle East correspondence to a Whitehall contact who suggested a modicum of caution in dealing with any country in the area that might again embark on a military adventure. This same man in the ministry also suggested that another approach be made to Saudi officials, who might be more responsive to discussing business if AEL were prepared to offer significant modifications to its vehicles. Given that George had spent months fruitlessly trying to cultivate senior Riyadh contacts, this change of heart by the Saudis came as something of a surprise to him.

But in the meantime, the Iraqi government appeared more anxious than ever to do business. And they didn't need much of a sales pitch either. Without much prompting, they settled on the top-of-the-range F-Series and were prepared to buy for bulk deliveries. Suddenly George found himself with an order worth £45 million spread over two years.

With the Iraqi order safely under its belt, AEL immediately noticed a perceptible shift in the Saudi negotiating position. Although they were still quite keen to modify existing designs they seemed intent, at first, on signing an agreement as quickly as possible. To George's mind, the Saudis had some rather daring ideas, one of which concerned the establishment of a local manufacturing company, which could be majority owned by the Saudis but run by AEL.

Months of negotiations ensued. On several occasions, it looked as if the talks would collapse over seemingly trivial matters that were beyond George. Perhaps their most exasperating feature was the Saudi insistence on acquiring only the very best technology or, better still, the next generation of technology.

Finding it increasingly difficult to persuade Saudi officials that AEL was offering them only the best available, George consulted Elinor in Mansfield. Between them they thrashed out an action plan that finally convinced Riyadh. And it all hinged on extending their design and production chains into the Middle East.

First of all, a computer link would be established between Mansfield and the new Riyadh factory. This on-line system would prove costly to install but it offered tangible proof that AEL was but a few key strokes away from any query that the

Saudis might have. In turn, a design team, assembled from existing AEL staff but augmented by local designers at a later date, would be located in the Saudi capital.

Mansfield's own computer-based design system had developed in quantum leaps since its troubled introduction in the earlier part of the decade. Now considered Elinor's pride and joy, which she demonstrated to any willing visitor, this vast network of VDUs occupied a central role in the running of AEL. Computer-aided design and manufacturing programmes and some quite exotic resource planning applications[1] had been concocted and were now offering entirely new approaches to the company's existing business.

Over the next two years, the Riyadh plant was meticulously planned and brought into operation. And with the resident design team looking at things from an entirely Saudi perspective, the shape of vehicle designs began to look quite different from anything Mansfield had seen before.

With complete autonomy over everything except budgets, the Riyadh team had decided quite early on to produce a new vehicle from scratch. Almost every evening in Mansfield, Elinor viewed the output from the Riyadh plant. On screen she saw emerge a whole host of new design permutations that were actively under consideration two thousand miles away.

Now instead of the familiar angular-shaped vehicles that Mansfield was producing, there emerged a softer, more rounded, form. With an upper body configuration that curiously resembled that of a turtle, the new vehicle was designed to enable it to 'burrow' into soft sand, leaving only a small portion of its armour visible. And in place of the normal four-wheel drive cum half-track assembly, Riyadh had devised a one-third track configuration with wheeled assemblies front and rear.

The team had also discovered some interesting things about the Saudi army's existing personnel carrier fleet. As a direct result of the harsh local climate, many key components in the vehicles failed. This epidemic among the personnel carrier fleet meant that at any given time, more than one-third of the vehicles were being repaired or serviced. By redesigning the vehicles' power train – the engine and transmission – the designers produced a more compact and modular engine assembly which allowed for rapid engine changes. Now that vehicles could be back on duty in a fraction of the time that existing servicing required, the effect was to raise the total size of the battle-ready fleet.

But Riyadh had even more revolutionary ideas in mind. One in particular meant asking the Saudi military to modify some basic assumptions on how they operated. The kernel of this idea was the creation of a four-vehicle platoon capable of transporting up to 50 soldiers into the heat of battle. Each vehicle would have a specific purpose, but each would retain sufficient similarity of components and design to allow interchangeability of operators and spare parts if necessary.

Of the four vehicles, one would act as a control centre, another would be armed with a heavy-duty gun, a third would have ambulance facilities and the fourth would perform solely as a troop carrier. The platoon's forward capability would be enhanced by being able to direct close-quarter airstrikes at enemy installations and still have sufficient firepower to fend off a counter-attack. On the other hand, its rear capability was reinforced by its ability to ferry wounded back to its own lines and bring up reinforcements.

With such a radical initiative in engineering design, Elinor wondered whether a similar industrial liaison with the British Army would produce results as impressive as these. Pushing these musings to the back of her mind, she remained content with the knowledge that here was a truly computer-designed military vehicle that would rival anything coming off the production line in Detroit.

Saudi government support for the project was unwavering and the Saudi Ministry of Defence seemed quite tickled with itself at having spearheaded such a novel approach to a new armoured corps. By early 1990, the first of these armoured vehicle platoons was accepted into Saudi defence forces and the Riyadh design team, already working on the next generation of designs, proudly unveiled their recently commissioned coat of arms and their new motto 'Faith in Engineering'.

But then the totally unexpected happened. As the first Saudi platoons were being put through their paces in the early part of 1990, initial rumblings of discord surfaced in the Iraqi government. By now fully re-equipped and possessing a military capability matched only by the Saudis and Israelis, the government of Saddam Hussein began adopting a more aggressive political posture in public.

By the summer, with the Baghdad rhetoric becoming more bellicose, Iraq's neighbours began to fear for their future. And what had seemed unthinkable only weeks earlier happened in August 1990 as the Iraqi army invaded Kuwait.

Once it became obvious that the western industrial countries were determined to intervene militarily in the Kuwait region, George and Elinor stepped up production of all military products in Mansfield and Riyadh. Now for the first time in its history, there was a real chance that one AEL vehicle model would be pitched against another in battle. Nothing had ever happened like this during the Second World War or the Falklands campaign. Not unsurprisingly it was an unnerving experience for everyone in Mansfield.

As the allies assembled their forces in Saudi Arabia for the recapture of Kuwait, George took up residence in Riyadh so he could monitor local production. By mid-January, with more than 700,000 Allied troops prepared for battle, the first part of the 'Desert Storm' campaign began with the aerial attack of Iraqi installations.

For the next five weeks, thousands of bombing raids were launched against Iraqi defence and communications targets in the hope that a land invasion would not be necessary. And finally, after repeated failed attempts at international diplomacy, the long-awaited 'Mother of all Battles' began on February 24, 1991.

Within hours of the Allies commencing their attack, it became apparent that the groundwork that they had done in previous months had paid off. Iraqi resistance, undermined by weeks of bombing, crumbled and what had begun as a tentative assault by the Allies turned into a high speed chase.

Given that the scale of the military intervention was so massive, it was proving difficult to single out individual weaponry. But Elinor, who had arrived in Riyadh shortly after the ground offensive began, was now intent on getting her hands, if possible, on a captured Iraqi armoured personnel carrier.

Within hours of the ground offensive being launched, the

first casualties were brought back. Although exceptionally light given the enormous scale of the military operation, the first wounded were debriefed by army officials. From one such cross examination, it transpired that several Iraqi army personnel carriers had been caught unexpectedly on the northern outskirts of al-Wafra. All had been destroyed.

Later that day, a Saudi military transport vehicle arrived in the area and, under the guidance of George, removed the shattered remains of a personnel carrier. Several hours later, in the relative security of a Saudi forward military base, Elinor, George and some of the Riyadh design team were looking at a burnt-out vehicle that had been manufactured in Mansfield less than three years earlier. To everyone's surprise, the shattered hulk of the F-Series personnel carrier in front of them was precisely that. A shattered hulk.

Elinor ordered an immediate investigation into the wreckage, and with the help of some Saudi military officials tried to determine what type of Allied weapon might have been used to destroy so completely a vehicle that most thought would have survived a direct hit. She now had to decide whether there was something unusual about the bomb that hit the personnel carrier or whether the vehicle had become weakened in some way.

Early factory analysis in Riyadh failed to find any significant clues. Elinor called the full design team together and checked through their regular test results. Everything suggested that the Saudi vehicles would have survived the impact of a similar explosion. But there was still something spectacularly wrong with the Iraqi personnel carrier, the remains of which had by now been dumped in the middle of an aircraft hanger south of the capital.

"It's the riddle of the sands," George joked with Elinor the following morning, the second full day of the Allied advance into Kuwait and Iraq.

"It's not funny, George," she snapped back. "We've got some irate customers here, and they want to know that their products are as safe as we claim. We've got to do something."

Assume, George instructed, that the regular Saudi quality test results were accurate. Assume also, he said, that the Iraqi vehicles, sourced in Mansfield, might not have been adequately maintained. "What I'm getting at Elinor is that we're not comparing like with like. Let's pull the wreck apart and see what we find." In the meantime, he suggested, she would have to assure the Saudi ministry that the AEL vehicles coming out of the Riyadh plant were more than a match for anything on the battlefield.

During the next two days, as the Allies moved closer to Baghdad, there was little that Elinor or George could do other than wait for field reports to come back and to watch CNN news programmes. Events were happening so rapidly, there was little chance to influence their direction.

The ground war, lasting little more than four days, saw the Pan-Arab Task Force flank the British 1st Armoured division in its drive into Kuwait. To the east, Saudi, Kuwaiti and Qatari troops made a coastal approach into the country, while the bulk of American forces pushed deep into Iraq. And within 100 hours it was all over. Kuwait had been recaptured.

By early March, as Kuwait's oil fields continued to burn out of control and the Iraqi city of Basra staged an uprising against Saddam Hussein, George and Elinor met in the relatively peace and tranquillity of the visitor's bar at the British base in Akrotiri in Cyprus.

The 'riddle of the sands' had been solved. Strangely enough, the poor performance of the Iraqi personal carriers had something to do with temperature. Although both the Iraqi and Saudi vehicle types were designed to operate in intense desert conditions, it transpired that the Saudi personnel carriers were assembled and subsequently maintained in air-conditioned factories. The Iraqi vehicles, assembled in Mansfield and shipped to the Middle East, were normally housed in wide open military compounds. This subtle difference in temperature proved enough to weaken some of the chemical bonds in the polyfibre panels. Purely by chance, the Saudi vehicles were inherently stronger.

George joked that with results like these, the vehicles could be indestructible in the Arctic.

With the Kuwaiti campaign safely behind them, Elinor told George it was now time to look to the future. Given that they had successfully survived this first post-Cold War crisis, they were in little doubt that AEL equipment would see service again soon. And with events taking a dramatic turn in the Soviet Union, the world was suddenly becoming a more dangerous and unpredictable place.

"While we've been fighting our desert war," she added, "Europe has changed. Germany is reunited and 1992 is just around the corner."

George nodded in agreement.

Raising her glass in a mock toast, Elinor joked: "You know George, I think it's time to unleash my daughter on the unsuspecting Europeans."

Chapter Notes

Against a backdrop of world recession, the early 1990s heralded the end of many old political conflicts and the coming together of old adversaries, first in Germany, and then later in the Middle East and South Africa. All these events, however, were overshadowed, or perhaps facilitated, by the collapse of the Soviet Union under Mikail Gorbachev. The political and economic upheaval caused by the demise of one of the Super Powers was to have long-lasting and largely unpredictable effects on the West.

In Germany, once the industrial powerhouse that kept the Western European economies moving, reunification was proving to be a mixed blessing. Although the political will to absorb the former German Democratic Republic remained intact, the country as a whole was paying a high economic price with rising unemployment and uncharacteristically high interest rates. And recession, a phenomenon not experienced by many young affluent Germans, would soon take the gloss off recent political achievements. Given that reunification was a major political milestone for which little social or economic planning could take place, Germany would spend most of the decade trying to assimilate what at times it felt were fundamentally disparate industrial and economic cultures within the new state.

In Britain, already deeply rooted in recession before the collapse of communism, things fared hardly any better. It was none the less hoped that German reunification, and the reduced threat of invasion from the Warsaw Pact countries, would yield a 'peace dividend' through defence spending cuts. Whatever benefits these cuts may have had on the economy as a whole, they had an immediate impact on the financial fortunes of many British engineering companies that had traditionally relied on MoD orders. A brief respite for the domestic, namely the European market, would be offered through defence replenishment in the aftermath of the Gulf War, but it would take an aggressive international sales campaign by British companies early in the decade before Britain became one of the largest suppliers of defence equipment in the world.

Reference Notes
[1]Elinor's rigorous approach to planning took her naturally from closed-loop material requirements planning through to MRP II, or manufacturing resource planning.

By using computer systems and manufacturing approaches based on MRP II she had effective planning and control of all AEL's resources, priorities and performance levels. This enabled her to produce the right quantity of high-quality products at the right time for her customer base. Central to the idea of MRP II is the concept of balancing supply (in the form of materials available and plant capacity) with demand for the finished product.

Chapter Sixteen – The Present

The white Porsche roared up Mainzer Landstrasse past the twin towers of the Deutsche Bank headquarters. Elena Dartry had not expected so much traffic on the road from Bad Homburg and she hoped, with a little luck, to be on time for the meeting.

She caught sight of her Uncle George pacing up and down the lobby of the Zukunft Turm as she gave the car keys to the parking attendant. Always a worrier, she thought.

"Elena!" George called out as she entered the revolving doors. "They're waiting."

"I hope you've fortified them with plenty of vodka," she joked.

George missed the humour entirely. "That'll come later, have you read the report? What do you think?"

She replied diplomatically. "Let's hear what they have to say first."

They rushed into the elevator and pushed the button for the 57th floor.

In the 12 years since her uncle had first suggested that she join the ranks of AEL, Elena, representing the third generation of Dartrys in the company, had undergone a thorough apprenticeship. A first class honours degree in robotics from Cranfield was followed by a lengthy secondment to Tri-State Engineering in New Jersey and a brief stint at the Harvard Business School, which she cut short on the grounds that AEL was awash with enough theory and practice to keep anyone going for a lifetime. A flair for languages – proficiency in French, German and Russian – earmarked her for a business career on the continent and when her mother had suggested in 1991 that she take control of their German interests and a budding Frankfurt distributorship, Elena grabbed the opportunity.

178

Now in her early thirties, she was one of the youngest, and most attractive, company directors in Germany and was making a distinct impression on the sober-minded, male-dominated Frankfurt business community. Elena claimed it was just a matter of good timing as anyone who knew what they were doing could make a fortune in a unified Germany. Her apparent run of good luck did not end there as eastern Europe, and then the Soviet Union, were suddenly opened up to free enterprise and market economies.

And now as the elevator doors whished open, Elena and her Uncle George were rushing into the AEL-Deutschland boardroom, where they were to meet a Russian delegation from the 4th State Vacuum Cleaner Plant in St Petersburg. In his role as roving ambassador for AEL, George had met the Russians several times in St Petersburg and had discussed at length AEL's management philosophy and the company's desire to expand even further eastwards.

With the bustling Frankfurt skyline as a backdrop, polite introductions were made, seats were shifted about, briefcase locks clicked open, papers rustled and then finally all was quiet.

"Miss Dartry," Alexander Chekhovich, leader of the grey-suited Russian delegates began. "If we may get down to business straight away. What is your answer to our proposal?"

Elena was a little taken aback by the no-nonsense approach of this pale-faced visitor with stilted English. She paused a moment and replied. "Of course, we are flattered that you should consider AEL-Deutschland for such a joint venture, but we would like to know why you picked us."

"We know your record, Miss Dartry, and how you have radicalised this company," Chekhovich responded.

"Our record is public knowledge, our techniques less so," George interjected.

"Exactly," Chekhovich expanded. "We have heard about your chains already. But we need *you* to put them into practice."

Elena continued: "I don't know whether we can help. Your terms are more than generous." In fact, the Russians were offering a one-third stake in their factory which employed more than 12,000 and had an annual turnover in excess of 600 million new roubles.

"If our terms are generous, why do you hesitate?" Chekhovich persisted. The Russian nervously pushed his glasses back onto the bridge of his nose and brushed his jet black hair off his forehead.

"Please don't misunderstand me," Elena said limply.

"Please be honest with us," Chekhovich rejoined quickly.

"You're right, we should be completely honest with you." Elena looked Chekhovich in the eye and continued: "Our chain theory has evolved during the past 65 years. It's not like a medicine you get from a doctor, take a mouthful and you're feeling alright."

George shuffled uneasily in his chair as his niece highlighted a few home truths.

"Our theory assumes certain conditions," she continued, "such as a market economy, capital markets, and a watertight belief in profit and loss accounts, brand names and intellectual property."

"We are not naive, Miss Dartry," Chekhovich insisted. "We simply want to know about your chains."

"There's no point in learning about these if you don't understand how western markets operate. You don't have a culture ready to work in these ways!" Elena heard her own voice rising higher than she wanted and immediately apologised to her Russian visitors for any discourtesy.

Shrugging off any slight, real or imagined, Chekhovich persisted: "Miss Dartry, we know the history of your company. Your uncle has entertained us for many hours with stories about your grandfather." Elena glanced at George.

"We know why it has developed in the way it did. We know how it moved with the tide of history yet created something special in British engineering."

"What's this got to do with our chains?" Elena inquired.

Chekhovich paused briefly, perhaps for dramatic effect. "In many ways," he said, "our company is like the firm that your grandfather founded during the 1920s. Our technology is much better now, of course, but the intellectual framework we operate in is rooted in the early days of the Soviet Union."

Elena looked the Russian squarely in the eye as he drew a deep breath.

Chapter Sixteen

"You spent 65 years building your chains," Chekhovich continued. "Well, we want to learn them, from start to finish. It might take us 10 years but certainly not 65 years." He returned Elena's hard gaze. "But, for you, it will be a challenge like you've never experienced. From what you've done with this German company, we think you can do the same for us, only on a much larger scale."

Elena thought momentarily about Chekhovich's quite eloquent speech which had hit at her weakest spot – her total belief in the Dartry chains. She looked sideways at George again, chuckled, and said: "Do you really understand what you are asking for?" She brushed the hair out of her face. "Do you know that it will mean changing not only the way you do things, but the way you think, the way you treat capital and time[1], how you meet the needs of the customer, that you produce what the market wants, not what you want?"

Solemnly, the Russians nodded.

"Right!" said Elena, "Let's start at the beginning with re-engineering your chains."[2]

Sweeping vistas, heroic landscapes, they were all there. In Elena's eyes, Russia possessed everything. Well virtually everything, except the ability to run a business efficiently.

Backed by a project team of four other Frankfurt-based staff, Elena had embarked on this Russian adventure brim full of optimism, tinged only with a little sense of trepidation. Russia, she convinced herself, had come a long way since the break-up of the Soviet Union in the 1991 revolution. Uncontrollable forces had been unleashed then and only now were some of them being harnessed to reshape this last great frontier in the northern hemisphere. No one knew for certain how the finished product, the new Russia, would turn out but Elena was sure that she wanted to play a part in it. And her part was about to begin in a southern suburb of St Petersburg, where the main factory of the 4th State Vacuum Cleaner Plant was located on the road to Kolpino.

Having installed her team in the absurdly expensive but safe Preobrazhenskii Hotel in central St Petersburg, Elena took a taxi to the factory where she was due to meet Alexander Chekhovich before the night shift took over. This was the same young Russian delegate who had talked her into this adventure a mere three months ago.

As the taxi lurched to a halt in front of a monolithic weather-beaten white-painted concrete structure, Elena wondered just how far back in time she had travelled. She had prepared herself for a bit of a let-down but not anything of this magnitude. First impressions count, she repeatedly told her Frankfurt staff. Now she was wondering how serious a mistake she had made in agreeing to come to St Petersburg.

Alex, as Chekhovich insisted on being called, was waiting at the front door."Well, what do you think?"

"I think I made a mistake."

Alex ignored her. "You see we've changed the name," he enthused. What had once been the 4th State Vacuum Cleaner Plant had been rechristened 'Elecktroprospekt'.

"How big is this place?"

"Roughly 60,000 square metres. Impressive, huh?"

Paying the taxi driver with new rouble notes and a dollar tip, she stood more in anguish than in awe of the building. "Sixty thousand square metres," she mused as she walked up the crumbling concrete steps to the reception area, "to make 100,000 vacuum cleaners a year. Well, Alex, we might have our work cut out for us after all."

For the next few days, Elena developed a simple routine. Early breakfast at the Preobrazhenskii Hotel was followed by the half-hour taxi drive to the Elecktroprospekt factory where she met senior managers, examined production plans and conducted unguided tours of the factory floors.

As a factory, Elecktroprospekt was typical of many Russian industrial enterprises created in the heyday of the Brezhnev era. The plant's functions were broadly divided into metal pressing, injection moulding, assembly and packing, card-board printing and tooling.

Given that she had already written off the metal pressing section of the business as being outmoded, Elena quickly moved into the plastic moulding facilities. In contrast to the near-derelict metal pressing shop, the layout and house-keeping in this area appeared reasonable although the management of scrap and the regrinding of reject material was manifestly inadequate even to an untutored eye.

Significantly, however, she sensed that the management in the plastic moulding section was above average and this might prove crucial at a later date.

Immediately offsetting this glimmer of hope was the large number of moulding machines that did not appear to be making components for vacuum cleaners. Elena already knew what components to look for, yet she could find hardly any that matched her design notes. Instead, she found that the majority, a good 45 of the 80 units in operation, were being used for subcontract work or other peripheral work for Elecktroprospekt.

Moving on to the two floors above, she found where final assembly of the company's vacuum cleaners took place. One floor each was assigned for the company's principal products, the Amba 1000 and the Viktor 2000. Here she noted that access for incoming materials to both assembly lines was haphazard, but more so for the Viktor 2000. In a factory that covered the area of several football fields, there were only four sets of goods lifts and of these only two served the top floor where the Viktor 2000 was assembled. Inexplicably, to Elena's way of thinking at least, there were also solid brick walls separating the assembly halls and the production offices. She made a note that glass partitions should be installed immediately.

Elsewhere she found a cardboard printing facility that appeared to be knee-deep in scrap paper and board. And its production seemed to be dedicated to Elecktroprospekt's output of plastic toys and to products made by other St Petersburg companies.

As for the tool-making facilities, there was good news and bad. Some of the machine tools were equal in quality to those in AEL's British plants but there were others so old and worn that they could not even operate within Elecktroprospekt's own rather lax performance range. Worse still was the duplication of machines with a dozen identical bar feed lathes in one area. Rationalisation of this equipment would have to become a priority, as would investment in new high-quality machine tools.

It was becoming obvious that great reliance was placed on the tool room machinists and fitters to produce enough good-quality tools as well as to repair any broken plant.

By the third day of this investigation, she was coming to terms with the reality of Elecktroprospekt – namely, that the enormity of the problem facing her was almost beyond comprehension. Just before going to lunch in the works canteen she called into Alex's underfurnished office for a heart-to-heart chat. Never prone to let people misunderstand, nor underestimate her, Elena didn't mince her words.

"Alex, I don't know where to begin. It's a quagmire. I simply didn't think such an industrial catastrophe could be squeezed into one firm. I'm at a loss where to start."

Alex looked at her calmly. "Do you want to quit?"

"I would love to quit, but I gave you my word I would help. You must understand there'll have to be an appalling upheaval in this company. Are you sure the workers can take it? Can *you* take it?"

"Elena, we didn't think we could save everything. But if we don't try to save some of it, we might lose it all. What do you want to do?"

"I need better data before I do anything drastic. Give me all your production programmes and commercial data. Take me through them all." A glum-looking Alex turned to his desk and started to make a telephone call.

"Oh, and by the way, let me have a look at your strategic business plan."

Alex's blank face rang alarm bells for Elena.

After lunch, Elena went on a second tour of the works that day. This one, instead of looking at the vacuum cleaner production area, was more concerned with the new paint and galvanising facility.

What perplexed Elena here was the apparent lack of co-ordination behind this project. Although a new building was under construction, almost finished in fact, the new painting equipment had already been set up. Most of it, however, had been left exposed to the harsh St Petersburg weather and was beginning to show signs of serious rust. There was also the nagging doubt in Elena's mind that the company didn't really need a new paint line, but had somehow managed to acquire one.

When she raised the subject later with Alex he explained

that good industrial facilities were proving difficult to obtain in the St Petersburg area and Elecktroprospekt had decided to take in as much subcontract work as possible to maintain its cash flow or broaden its barter possibilities. When he then told her about the toy-making machinery they had acquired last year, she cracked.

"You make it sound as if you're a mini-conglomerate," Elena snapped. "But you're not, you make vacuum cleaners, and the sooner you understand that the better."

"I am not sure that I agree," Alex said rather stiffly.

Elena was startled by what she viewed as insolent behaviour. She obviously had rankled Alex with her last remark and now decided to slow the pace down slightly. "You make electric domestic cleaning equipment."

Alex nodded in agreement. "But we also make plastic components, toys, and ..."

Elena cut him short: "Let me ask you a simple question. How much do you make on the plastic components or the toys? How profitable are they"

"I don't know. But I could find out."

"If you don't know whether you're making money, why are you making the stuff?" Alex, biting his lower lip for a moment, nodded again in agreement.

"There is another problem we have to talk about." Elena hesitated slightly before she raised the matter of investment. "AEL promised to inject some capital into this company, but quite honestly the sums needed here are astronomical. You could bankrupt us. What we need to do is find fresh capital. Maybe 50 or 60 million new roubles."

"That may be a problem but I think we should be able to get most of it."

Elena looked dumbfounded. "Where can you find that sort of money? You've got virtually nothing here."

"Oh, we have our factories, or reserves, our farms."

"Alex, you make vacuum cleaners, don't worry about farming."

"But that's how we pay some of our suppliers. We exchange goods. We barter our production when we cannot get cash." Suddenly sounding hurt and on the defensive, Alex continued: "Elena, we would not have approached you if we were destitute. We have ways of getting capital, don't worry, but please do not criticise something that you may not have tried yourself."

"Okay, you show me how we are going to get 50 million roubles."

"Well, it depends on the season of course."

Not entirely sure she had heard Alex correctly, Elena shook her head in disbelief. "What do the seasons have to do with it?"

"Everything," Alex said firmly. He then explained that sometime during the 1970s, senior management had exchanged 20,000 vacuum cleaners for land in Siberia. The land was seen as 'income producing' because of the fur trade and forests. And it had proved to be a good investment in that they were still getting a return from the land.

"How much land?" Elena asked pointedly.

He picked out his Braun pocket calculator with a flourish and pressed several keys. "About one million acres."

"And you have clear title to this land?"

Alex nodded his head vigorously. "Indisputable."

Elena wanted to reassure herself on a few matters. "And how much income does it produce?"

"About 2,000 pelts are shipped out of Igarka each spring. And 40,000 acres of pine forests are cut and replanted every year. But there might also be some geological prospects."

"What do you mean?"

"Shell and Exxon want to buy exploration rights. This, of course, has to be done with the consent of the national and regional governments. But a one-million-acre exploration concession is worth something to the Americans and the Dutch.

Elena returned to the prime issue as she saw it. "So how do you propose to get our 50 million roubles?"

Unperturbed, Alex outlined his plan: "Sell the forests in one lot, and maybe sell the exploration rights as well. If we are to concentrate on making electrical appliances we won't need the timber income in future years, No?"

"Yes, you're right."

"Good; that is settled then. We sell the forests. But we may have to barter them for oil before we can exchange them into utmost surprise, Elena now discovered that the agent Alex proposed to use on the barter contract was none other than her father Anthony Fairfax.

Fairfax, having spent most of the previous 15 years building up a vast network of barter clients throughout the Soviet Union, had hardly set foot out of the Comecon trading bloc. When the Soviet system finally collapsed in 1991, he found himself in the enviable position of being one of the few Westerners whom local businessmen could implicitly trust.

For both Elena and her mother Elinor, Anthony Fairfax had developed into a truly enigmatic figure. Notwithstanding the years of absence and obvious neglect, Elena would, in time, get to know this tall cryptic man who had remained such a mysterious figure in her life.

Most immediately, however, Elena had to concentrate on saving this dilapidated vacuum cleaner factory.

Pulling a sheet of paper from her briefcase, Elena slid it across to Alex. It contained a sketch of two simple Design and Manufacturing chains, with the four levels of Strategic, Tactical, Operational and Continuous running down the middle.

"We start with the basics," she said, "and that means looking at how the company operates and how the existing chains run through it. Then we strengthen them."

Alex looked perturbed. "Is that it?"

"Yes," she smiled, "as simple as that. Every function in the design and production of your business is, or can be, included on a chain diagram. It's like a road map to better manufacturing. It shows you the main routes you have to follow, but also some short-cuts if you get caught up in traffic.

"Elena, when we first met in Frankfurt, you told us we would have to undergo a cultural change. Our way of thinking would need to be more market, market...?"

"Market-oriented?" Elena suggested.

"Yes, market-oriented," he said. "Well, I think it is possible to use these chains to create this."

Elena looked surprised. "What do you mean?"

"It is simple. Your four parts of the chain can be used to create a commercial culture." Elena tilted her head in anticipation.

"I think we have to develop your Design and Manufacturing chains with another one. You may not find it necessary in your country but for Russia, for St Petersburg and for Elecktroprospekt at the moment, it is necessary. The starting point of *our* chain must be management culture, then we can use the four links in your chain." Not entirely sure what he was getting at, Elena none the less nodded agreement.

"You told me in Frankfurt that we should be looking at things in a totally different way now, and that is what we are doing," he explained. "You might not have to worry about basic company law in Britain or in Germany, but we do. Will we be a PLC someday, or a partnership or a collective? These are strategic management issues for us."

Nodding slowly in agreement, Elena could see that Alex was beginning to understand the philosophy behind the Dartry chains. And she was starting to learn something about how the Russian mind analysed problems.

"Elecktroprospekt," he continued, "cannot even begin to think about your chains until we get this one right first."

It was agreed that Alex would now devote himself solely to this new part of the design and manufacturing chains while Elena tried to find a sensible place from which to start the reorganisation, or the 're-engineering' as she called it, of the vacuum cleaner factory.

In truth, the Elecktroprospekt factory was in such a shambles she didn't know where to begin. So she started with the most obvious. She changed the name of the company again, but this time gave it a vaguely Western European sound to it. The name 'Elecktroprospekt' was killed off in favour of 'Electropros', which now suggested an air of prosperity linked with electrical goods. Even if the name looked a tad like 'Electrolux', they could be forgiven for that slight indiscretion. Anyway, Elena rationalised, there was hardly any chance of confusion between the two companies. So much for cosmetics. Now onto the real job at hand.

In Elena's view, Electropros suffered a number of significant structural shortcomings. In product terms, its technology was outdated. Worse still, its process technology was also rooted in the mid-1970s. Elena had already discovered that whereas most of the international manufacturers of vacuum cleaners had moved to plastic components, Electropros' products were still essentially based on metal parts. And the greatest crime lay in the company's motors. This essential power unit had been consistently manufactured to low standards with the result that its power ratings were significantly less that international rivals.

Elena requisitioned the production data on the company's two main vacuum cleaners. Hoping to find some clues, she found only disturbing reading. There wasn't enough time to prepare other fresh data so she began visiting the factory floor more often. Here the situation was equally grim.

As Elena poked her head into every nook and cranny in the building, Alex made rapid progress with his creation of a management culture theory. If in doubt about some aspect of his work, he would take himself off to the cocktail bar of the Conrad Hotel, where he would pick the brains of the resident army of foreign businessmen and consultants that had invaded St Petersburg since the early 1990s. With professional back-up like this, Alex felt confident enough in less than a week to tell Elena about his findings. So much so that he offered to give her a preview of the formal presentation that he intended making to Elecktropros's management.

With childlike enthusiasm, he arrived with his coloured pencils and sketches in Elena's spartan office one morning. And with his back to the door, he commenced.

"I have entitled this presentation *In Search of a Management Culture*," he said rather stiffly.

"Loosen up," Elena suggested, "feel at ease with yourself and you'll convince your audience quicker."

Alex began again. "I've called this presentation *Management Culture*."

"Much better," Elena encouraged.

He flipped over a page of the display to reveal:

Management Culture

STRATEGIC

1) Board of Directors
   2) Business mission
      3) PLC??

"As a consumer goods business in post-Soviet Russia, we must examine new commercial structures," he began. "A prerequisite of these is the creation of a board of directors. This board will include a managing director, elected by other members of the board. He will have responsibility for developing a business strategy and for managing six other directors. These six board members will have responsibility for Operations, Supplies, Sales and Marketing, Engineering, Finance, and Personnel." He paused briefly and pointed to the second item on his chart.

"Each director will be expected to carry out the company's 'business mission' in his or her own area. This business mission will be a clearly stated public declaration of what the company hopes to do.

"A further strategic feature of the culture will be the legal framework we operate under. Will Electropros be a public limited company, or a large-scale partnership, or some other suitable form of organisation? This crucial issue will be resolved by the board of directors."

Elena nodded her head in agreement. Alex now turned his flip chart to reveal the tactical part of the management chain.

Management Culture

TACTICAL

1) Search for new capital
2) Privatisation
3) Consultants

"We must acquire new capital," he went on. "Some progress has been made with the sale of timber reserves but we will need to look at other ways of raising capital." Elena interrupted him briefly by suggesting that he stop making a speech. Give them ideas, Alex, she urged, they'll put the ideas into their own words.

"One possibility," he continued, "of course, may be through a partial privatisation of the company, but this only makes sense if we are allowed to keep some of the proceeds to re-invest in the company."

"Bravo," Elena cheered from the sidelines.

"It might be possible to sell a stake in the company in exchange for advice, much like what we have done with AEL, but there is a limit to how far we can do this."

"Touché," Elena replied, "Perfectly right and well argued."

Buoyed by her comments, Alex seemed more confident as he revealed the next part of his chain.

Management Culture

OPERATIONAL

1) Financial controls
  2) Licensing
    3) Seminars
      4) Industrial espionage

"Fostering a new management culture at this level of the chain means how we perform our daily chores. Are we capitalists or communists?" He paused for dramatic effect. "We are, in fact, neo-capitalists competing against entrenched capitalists who have a 75-year head start over us. We must learn their skills, use their tools to master our own society."

Good sense of history, Elena thought to herself.

"We'll need effective financial controls in the company, controls that are every bit as good as those in the West. We'll need to start licensing products and technology until we can stand on our own two feet."

Seminars, conferences, discussion groups, all these would have to raise the calibre of our managers, Alex claimed. Nodding in agreement, Elinor now enquired what did the item 'industrial espionage' mean?

"That is a little joke," he confided "We need to know more about what our competitors are doing, so I thought since everyone has experienced the KGB in some form, industrial espionage might emphasise the point."

"Nice idea," she admitted "but be careful you don't have

any genuine spy masters doing the work for you."

"Finally," he said, "if we are behaving like a modern management, we need to constantly conduct our affairs in an orderly way. This means annual general meetings, shareholders representations and probably paying them dividends at some stage. And like any good management we will be constantly looking at the key business issues affecting our industry."

With this last comment, Alex revealed his last placard.

Management Culture

CONTINUOUS

1) AGM
  2) Dividends?
  3) Critical business issues

Rising from her desk, Elena beaming the smile of a satisfied teacher, shook Alex's hand and congratulated him on a job well done. "You've cracked it," she said, "you've applied our chain theory to something that we never even thought about. It's remarkable, you've maintained the logical progression throughout. I'm very impressed. Our only concern now is whether your colleagues will warm to it also."

Over the following weeks, as Alex fine-tuned his presentation, Elena had reached her own conclusion about the future of the Electropros business. She now called a meeting of the company's top two dozen managers, people who ranged from Kholmiansky, head of the tooling department, to Jurovsky who was in charge of barter.

The purpose of the meeting was to explain in detail the proposals that Elena had formulated. And as a preliminary to Elena's more far-reaching analysis, Alex would make his presentation on the creation of a new management culture within Electropros. Thus it was hoped he would set the mood and get the managers familiar with a coherent logical approach to business life. Once this had been established, Elena would then commence her detailed presentation of the design and manufacturing chains. She knew it would not be an easy meeting because what she intended proposing was the virtual destruction of the existing company.

On the appointed day, two dozen senior managers, clutching clipboards and pencils, gathered in the small meeting room. Almost like a first night at the opera, there was a sense of anticipation in the air. And with Elena sitting quietly at the back of the room, Alex duly gave a tour de force. Elena was genuinely impressed at his polished approach which would not have been out of keeping in any Western boardroom. As for the company's managers, they hung on his every word. Ferocious note-taking was occasionally interrupted with lucid questions and cogent remarks. At the end, the managers rewarded Alex with a thoroughly well-deserved round of applause.

Slowly the managers quietened down and Elena made her way to the front of the room. At last, her moment of truth had arrived. Having already decided to start the talk off slowly, Elena, speaking in Russian, reminded the managers that her own parent company had developed its engineering theory over three generations and that, as Alex had shown, there was room for further development.

In stark contrast to the ebullient mood just a few moments earlier, these comments were greeted with a stony silence that alerted Elena to an underlying hostility. Keep calm, she told herself, and they'll warm up to the idea soon enough. She explained that during this morning session she intended to look at the Design Chain in the company and, after lunch, they would study the manufacturing side of the business. She continued. "One of the first things that struck me," she said slowly, "was the absence of product strategy in this firm." She paused.

"Without a clear product strategy," she announced, "you will find it difficult to align business plans with future market requirements."

Unexpectedly, a hand was raised near the back. She had not bargained on a question and answer session but decided to take the query. A burly man with a tight fitting grey suit stood up. He introduced himself as Khabalov, head of the design department. How, he wanted to know, could anyone have a product strategy if there was doubt whether the factory would be in business a year from now.

Elena stuck to the textbook answer at first: "Your range of vacuum cleaners lacks definition and there is considerable overlap between your products." Khabalov remained standing, so Elena picked up with a more aggressive tack. "Your product strategy doesn't react to market opportunity. Instead, your manufacturing and design capability dictate what is made. You have it the wrong way around."

"Without a product strategy," she continued, "your company will certainly perish. With one, it might survive. I am sorry to be so blunt."

Pleased with himself for having elicited such an honest answer, Khabalov sat down and Elena picked up the threads of her talk. "The next stage," she resumed, "is to stop making products that don't fit into your new strategy. Does anyone really want to buy a replacement for the Viktor 2000 if it isn't much better than the machine they already have? Until you can make something better, you'll need to start licensing foreign designs that fit into your product strategy."

A voice from the middle of the room now interrupted her. Why, the man asked, should they start making new models if they could sell all of their current production?

Deciding that the blunt approach had already paid dividends, Elena politely but firmly told her interrogator that even in Western economies current sales were no guide to future demand. The experience of the Comecon countries showed that once disposable income increased, market expectations soared. You must plan designs for the future, she finally suggested. Foreign designs, she warned, would only act as a stop-gap, a temporary plugging of a market opening.

"Your next strategic design element will be your ability to cut design lead times. At the moment, they're eighteen months to two years, yes?"

The head of the design department nodded his agreement.

"You must cut them to under a year!"

A man – Elena thought it was Gregoski from the engineering department – stood up immediately. "Is this done in Britain?"

"Yes," Elena replied.

"It is not possible!" Gregoski asserted "Not here."

"What makes you so special?" Elena rudely asked. "Why can you not meet international standards of design? You have the men, all good men, you have some good equipment, what's wrong? All you need to know is how it's done, that's all." Gregoski grunted and sat down, but Elena pursued him, reminding him of how American and European industry were aghast at the design prowess of the Japanese. We didn't think it could be done, she said, but we're doing it now ourselves.

"While you're cutting your lead times," she resumed, "you might as well switch from metal to plastic components." This last suggestion had the effect of throwing the room into near turmoil. Elena later likened their reactions to asking a Cordon Bleu chef to learn how to cook without using butter or wine.

Undismayed by their reaction, she continued."So, our first element of the design chain looks like this." She unfurled a large sheet of paper from a flip chart standing on a nearby wooden easel to reveal the following to the agitated group of managers:

Design

STRATEGIC

1) Develop a product strategy
   2) Cut out own redundant models
      3) License foreign designs
         4) Cut design lead times to maximum 1 year
         5) Move towards plastics

As the managers made notes of the chart Elena turned to Alex, who was sitting beside the easel. What, she asked, had got into them? She had never seen a reaction like this before. Professing ignorance, Alex promised he would find out, but she must continue the presentation.

Taking a long sip of water, Elena surveyed her antagonists.

She would just have to tough it out, she thought, just give it to them straight. If they didn't like it, that was their problem.

"Now let's look at Tactics," she announced. The room suddenly fell silent. "Your first tactical move must be to simplify your designs. You've already started to do this in some areas, but it must be done everywhere. The Amba 1000 model has 240 components and the Viktor 2000 has 160. In addition, the Amba has 10 different types of fixings including six different sizes of screw."

More than a few heads turned in surprise.

"Furthermore, no attempt has been made to use common components in the Viktor 2000. We have another totally different set of fixings and parts. This is the next aspect of design tactics. You must increase the inter-changeability of your components."

Two dozen managers were now unsettled. Their body language told Elena she was in trouble, that this amount of shifting about of torsos and mopping of brows meant only one thing, namely outright rejection. It's funny, she thought, she never imagined that her chain theory could be rejected. But now she seemed to be staring at disbelief in the faces of these senior managers. She knew, however, that if she hesitated, or showed any sign of weakness, she was lost. She pushed on.

"While you're trying to figure out how to use similar parts, you'll need to examine the heat endurance of the plastics you use. We've already decided to use more plastic, that's a strategic issue. Now tactically we must use a better plastic.

"The final tactical element you need to study now is the energy efficiency of your motors."

She paused again. "Energy conservation is not an important issue now, but within a few years, high energy costs in domestic housing will make it crucial. Improve your motors now for the market that will be there by the turn of the century."

Blenovich, from the tool room raised his hand as Elena turned the page on the flip chart to reveal the tactical design chain.

Design

TACTICAL

1) Simplify design
   2) Increase interchangeability of components
      3) Improve heat endurance
         4) Increase energy efficiency of motors

"Yes, Mr Blenovich."

"We cannot get enough parts even to make inefficient motors," he explained. "I must express some surprise that you now want us to make something of this nature." Elena was grateful for Blenovich's moderate tone. She responded in an equally measured manner.

"Imagine for a moment," she began, "being able to make a motor that was as good as anything coming out of Bosch or AEG. Then imagine being able to make it cheaper than anyone in Germany. You might not have a market for the motor in Russia, but you could start selling into the German market. Hard currency flows in, your domestic reputation is enhanced and you are light years ahead of the Russian competition."

Thank God Blenovich was responding to this, Elena thought.

Blenovich then quietly suggested to Elena that what she was implying was the market would exist if Electropros unilaterally improved its products.

"Exactly!" Elena agreed. "You've got it!" Hoping that Blenovich's enlightenment would spread to the others, she stepped up the pace. But her hopes proved to be unfounded.

Operational design, the next part of the chain, meant designing better products in a better fashion, she explained. By way of illustration she produced a table of the amount of assembly time required for three features of the Viktor 2000 model.

Viktor 2000	
Feature	*Assembly time (% of total)*
Automatic cable rewind	35%
'Bag full' indicator	10%
Dust collection bag	2%

"So, gentlemen," she smiled, "it appears to take 45 per cent of total assembly time to add two features that, from my research, don't seem to work very well anyway. This is because the cable rewind mechanism has 55 parts and the 'bag full' indicator has another 20 components. Both of these are too complex to make, which means they're unreliable and give the product a bad name." Relishing the moment, she drove the point home harder. "For those of you who enjoy football, this is an own goal."

There was an audible murmur of discontent among the managers at the latest revelation. Good design, Elena restated, sells products and from now on extra effort should be made to sell products on the strength of their design.

"Now I want to give you something else to think about," Elena resumed. "I discovered that the metal housings for each month's production arrive near the end of the month. We don't know how many we will get, nor do we know what colour they will be. Keep it simple. Make the vacuum cleaners in grey and only grey."

Jurovsky, head of the barter department, stood up. Housings had always been difficult to obtain, he explained, and it was only through years of forbearance had they been able to get enough supplies. His department was at the mercy of other suppliers.

"Wishing you no disrespect Mr Jurovsky," Elena replied, "but I think this company relies too heavily on barter. We are a customer to these suppliers. If they cannot give us what we want, we will take our business elsewhere. I suggest you tell them this, and you'll see a radical change in their attitude."

Jurovsky didn't know whether or not to feel insulted with

the answer so sat down anyway. Elena had by now unveiled the next stage of the chain.

Design

OPERATIONAL

1) Sell on design merits
2) Use a single colour

"Now, we're getting somewhere," she said. "I hope you can see how the strategic and tactical sections of the chain lead to here. Once you have reached this point, you need to keep doing all these earlier things to maintain the chain. And that leads us to the final component which we call 'Continuous'." Market research, she suggested, was one way of checking that the company was meeting customer expectations. But given the cost of such research and the state of the company, this should be postponed.

"But another, cheaper way," Elena proposed, "is to get feedback from existing customers. We want to know what works and what doesn't, whether our products are good enough to be recommended to friends, would an existing customer buy another one, if not, then find out the reason." She paused briefly, directed her attention to the flip chart once more and, turning over the final page of the Design Chain, asked the managers if there were any further questions.

Design

CONTINUOUS

1) Market research
2) Feedback from customers

Almost immediately, a dozen hands were raised and some senior managers began cross-examining Elena, who was genuinely taken aback by their reaction.

The pace of questioning was relentless. How could they train new designers, they asked, when they couldn't even keep their existing personnel? Where do they find the resources for proper certification of products? Was there any *real* need for product families? Did Russian citizens really care about brand name vacuum cleaners?

And so it went on for more than an hour. The aggressive, uncompromising tone of the interrogation drained Elena. Finally, she told them she needed to pause for a lunch break or she would not be able to continue in the afternoon. Fatigued by the unremitting cross-examination, she closed the door behind her and walked in the direction of the canteen and the smell of stewed cabbage. Just as she found a seat and was aimlessly stirring a cup of coffee, Alex caught up with her.

"What's wrong with them, Alex?" she implored. He shrugged his shoulders.

"But they were so aggressive..." she continued.

Alex remained silent for a moment or two. As he stared into his cup of coffee, he tried to make Elena understand. "I'm not sure if I can explain it. Maybe it's just something to do with being Russian."

"Try me," retorted Elena.

"Well, there is a certain pride, a Russian pride that has been injured," he suggested. "Don't worry, it has nothing to do with you. You are just telling them some home truths. You see Elena, they've worked hard, very hard to achieve things, and everything just came tumbling down." Elena looked perplexed.

"They know their vacuum cleaners are not very good, but that was all they could make for years," he said. "They weren't allowed to make anything better, the system proved too overpowering. When they complain, they're not complaining about you or the chains, they're hitting out against a system that put them in this mess in the first place."

"You mean they resent their former leaders?"

"In a sense, yes," Alex continued, "but in a way they resent me for having brought you here."

For the first time in years, Elena looked, sounded and felt hurt. "Are you saying they have a problem with me?"

"It's only a matter of presentation. No, they don't resent

you. They welcome you and your ideas but they need some confidence building, they need to feel *they* are in control of their destiny." Elena stared into her coffee cup. She asked Alex what did he suggest.

"Give them a chance," he said, "to find their own feet. Show them a completed chain for manufacturing and let them figure out what to do."

"I'm not sure they'll be able to follow it," Elena replied limply.

"If they make a mess of it, we'll sit them down again and you can go through it yourself. Remember you said the chains were like a road map to better manufacturing, give them your map and let them find their way."

Hesitantly, Elena opened her briefcase and extracted three documents which she passed to Alex.

Mission Statement

Electropos manufactures a range of internationally competitive vacuum cleaners and technologically compatible products for the Russian market.

Factory Space Requirements

Function	Estimated needs (m²)	Available	Surplus
Administration	2,000	4,600	2,600
Plastic moulding	1,500	5,000	3,500
Assembly	2,200	7,500	5,300
Tool room	1,000	5,000	4,000
Storage	3,000	7,000	4,000
Total	**9,700**	**29,100**	**19,400**

Manufacturing

STRATEGIC

1) Formulate mission statement
2) Close two-thirds of factory
3) Close peripheral activities
4) Reduce reliance on barter
5) Improve purchasing
6) Establish own distribution

TACTICAL

1) Lease vacant factory space, keep ground floor
2) Change layout of remaining factory
3) Introduce computer system
4) International testing standards

OPERATIONAL

1) Improve materials handling
2) Improve information flows
3) Create a unified warehouse
4) Introduce strict quality audits

CONTINUOUS

1) Just-in-time material deliveries
2) Increase own manufacture of components
3) Revise pay structures

"Blessed Virgin of Kazan!" Alex exclaimed, "Is this it? Just three pages?"

"Yes, that's all it'll take," Elena replied , "and if you're sure you want to do this, I'm going for a walk. I'll meet you back here in a couple of hours." Alex gathered up Elena's notes and, wishing himself luck, went back to the meeting room.

For her part, Elena suddenly looked forward to an afternoon

off and, once she had deposited her briefcase back in her office, she left the Electropros building with a lightness in her step that she had not known in several weeks. During the next couple of hours, she ambled part of the way back towards St Petersburg. Industrial blight was evident everywhere she looked. Run-down factories, some recently gutted by fire and others just falling apart, stood like sets on a Hollywood 'B' movie, hoping that someone would find a use for them in the future.

Finding herself increasingly depressed by the sight of the industrial decay, she waited at a bus stop for about a half hour with other hopeful passengers until a bus arrived. By 4 o'clock she was back inside the Electropros building, where she made her way back to the canteen expecting to find Alex.

The canteen was empty save for some kitchen staff preparing dinner for the night shift and the ubiquitous smell of freshly cooked cabbage. Notwithstanding this, Elena bought herself a coffee and a small piece of cake which she ate as she flicked through a copy of an old newspaper. Lost in thought, she did not notice the canteen staff manager approach her table. Every pore of this large well-fed woman seemed to ooze with the smell of cabbage. It was this concentration of odour that alerted Elena someone was standing beside her. Mr Chekhovich, she was told, had telephoned the canteen and asked that Elena return to the meeting room. Elena thanked the canteen manager and tidied away the newspaper. Wetting her index finger, she picked up the remaining crumbs of the cake and headed back through the long labyrinthine network of corridors.

A few minutes later, she stood outside the meeting room and, taking a deep breath, she turned the handle on the door and entered. The little buzz of conversation that had been in the room died away immediately. As she walked the few yards to the front, all two dozen managers stood up and began clapping.

She took her place at the top of the room, and flanked by the easel on one side and Alex on the other, she modestly nodded acceptance of their applause. The clapping continued and doubtless would have for much longer had Elena not signalled that the managers return to their seats. By now totally confused but none the less a little flushed with excitement, she waited for silence and asked what was the reason for such an outburst.

Alex stood up and on behalf of the managers explained that they had spent the previous three hours examining her pages of notes, which he now held up in full view to the entire room. In her absence, they had followed the path of her manufacturing chain.

"You mean you understand it all? Everything that needs to be done?" she asked.

From the grinning faces and nodding heads ranged in front of her, it looked like the managers thought they knew what needed to be done to turn the company around. Alex suggested that if she did not believe them she should ask questions. With the verbal roasting she received that morning still fresh in her mind, Elena gladly accepted the challenge. Looking at the chain diagram in front of her, she picked an element of the chain at random. She homed in on pay structures, the final item in the continuous phase of the chain.

Vorontsov, in charge of personnel, was the first with his hand up. Improving pay levels, he said, could be considered either a strategic element or a continuous component of the chain. Strategically, it was important to pay competitive wages for managerial as well as shop-floor workers. But because it was something that could not be achieved overnight, the company had to devise a continuous programme of pay reviews, perhaps linked to productivity. One possible shortcut, he suggested, would be to let it become known that the company intended to pay good rates for good work. This might persuade some workers who were thinking of leaving to stay longer, and it could well attract good staff from outside.

Impressed, Elena thanked him for his lucid comments. She now asked if there were any thoughts on the strategic issue of reducing barter.

Jurovsky, the head of the barter department who had proven so antagonistic earlier in the day, stood up. Barter acts as a substitute for cash, he pronounced. Although there is nothing inherently wrong with barter, he said, it is unsuitable when it begins to affect the quality of the products that are made. Given that cash creates better leverage over suppliers, cash generation and cash flow are crucial parts of the chain.

"If we need to barter our finished products," he concluded, "we must convert our goods received immediately into cash so the rest of the company may benefit."

"A very cogent argument, Mr Jurovsky, thank you." Elena now turned to the matter of factory space. She had envisaged the closure of two-thirds of the present factory, but wondered whether this had really been accepted.

Alex took up the issue. Yes, he said, it was difficult to see so much space go idle but since there was a chance of renting it, then it made economic sense to do so. This closure of unnecessary factory space, like the rest of the chain, was hard to accept but there were no easy options for the company at this point.

"And distribution?" Elena asked, "you see the need to distribute your own production?"

There appeared to be full agreement. A quick scrutiny of the tactical and operational parts of the chain confirmed this. Even the potentially sticky issues of computer systems and new warehousing were fully understood and accepted in principle. Trying one more time, Elena asked about quality audits.

The murmur of approval astounded her. It looked like they had done it. Alex had been right. They didn't need to be spoon-fed, they needed to do it themselves. It was simply a matter of Russian pride.

Flushed with this success, Elena felt there was little more she could do. So she thanked her audience for being so diligent and forthright in their questioning. But before she could gather up her papers, the room suddenly became a cauldron of noise and chatter with the managers pushing back chairs and swapping jokes. It had an end-of-term feeling to it. And when the canteen staff manager wheeled in a trolley packed full of English bottled beer and Russian vodka, there was a loud cheer from the managers. What ensued was a celebration not only of Elena's chains but of their own newly-found commercial freedom to operate as managers.

In the course of the early evening, as Elena stood sentinel-like in the middle of the floor, each Electropos manager approached her in turn and thanked her for helping them. Just wait, said one, you won't recognise this factory within six months. Another, in charge of tooling, gleefully rubbed his hands in anticipation of what he felt he could now achieve. If we all pull together, he told Elena, we can save the company. And so it went on. Each manager kindling a small precious flame of optimism where none existed before. It would be up to Alex and the other managers to coax this glimmer of hope into something more substantial and self-perpetuating. For the moment, Elena felt she had accomplished all that she had set out to achieve and it was now time to return to Frankfurt.

She asked for a taxi to be called, and within an hour she was sitting in her room at the Preobrazhenskii Hotel. And for the first time since she was in the St Petersburg hotel, she opened up the glass doors on her balcony and looked at the milling street life several floors below her.

She poured herself what she deemed to be a well-earned glass of Georgian champagne and as twilight descended on the city she cast her mind back to the odd chain of events that had brought her here. She wondered what her grandfather Tom Dartry, a staunch anti-communist if ever there was one, would think of her now in the former city of Leningrad and how she had managed to salvage a chronically-run Russian vacuum cleaner factory all because of his chain theory.

Topping up her glass one more time, Elena reached for her tape cassette player and pushed the START button.

And as she stared thoughtfully into the evening sky, the sounds of the Beatles singing "Chains! You've got me locked up in chains..." floated across the St Petersburg skyline.

Chapter Notes
The break-up of the Soviet Union, together with the collapse of the Warsaw Pact military alliance and the Comecon trading bloc, represented one of the greatest upheavals of the twentieth century, directly affecting the political and economic lives of almost 400 million people. From the West's point of view, Russia and the other major constituents of the former USSR now emerged as one of the greatest challenges and opportunities that any capitalist could hope to encounter. In Western eyes, decades of political dogma had

fossilised huge sections of the former communist economies and these were now deemed ripe for rapid development.

In the event, the least successful Westerners in the former Soviet Union would be those who attempted to impose capitalist orthodoxy on unwilling local managements. It would soon become evident that the Western philosophical approach to market economies would need to be administered in stages rather than dispensed on a wholesale basis. In fact, it would become abundantly clear that the creation of a management culture within the former USSR would prove to be one of the first, and perhaps most important, stepping stones to establishing a new economic order.

Reference Notes

[1]Elena was alluding to time-based management, an approach to improving operational performance that emerged in the US in the late 1980s. The basic theory grew from the JIT concept which required shorter manufacturing lead times and Total Quality production. In time-based management, time is considered as a valuable asset which should be used and measured with care. It also focuses on cycle times in all operational activities and the achievement of 'on-time' delivery. The early work on TBM was described in *Time Based Competition* by George Stalk. Later, businesses brought together the ideas of Total Quality and Time Based Competition to form the TBM approach which has been widely adopted to improve customer service.

[2]By the early 1990s, it became apparent that if companies were to achieve quantum leaps in performance, a fundamental overhaul of corporate structures, culture and technologies would be necessary. Such re-engineering and redesign were intended to take management thinking beyond accepted philosophies such as continuous improvement and TQM and heralded attempts to 're-invent' businesses (cf. *Business Process Reengineering*, Johansson, McHugh, Pendlebury and Wheeler; Wiley, 1993).

Appendix
"Morris Motors from the Inside"
(Feature article in *The Financial Times*, May 12, 1947)

Impressions of Cowley

"The Cowley factory of Morris Motors compresses into its two hundred-odd acres most of the problems which concern British industry today. There is the labour problem of productivity and supply. There is the shortage, notorious in all industrial towns, of housing accommodation. There is the constant worry whether the flow of materials drawn from many industries in different parts of the country will all be maintained, for a check in the supply of one might stop or slow down the whole production line.

Perfect Test Piece

"Cowley, in fact, is almost a perfect test piece. Its production is an indication of the activity in the engineering industry, of the availability of steel, textiles, timber, paint, hides – and so on. The rate at which cars come off the line is also an indication of the effort with which labour could work. That rate is quite high today; it has just been raised to about double that of a year ago. But it is still well below that what the plant can do, and did before the war. For those who own Morris shares, for those who want to own a Morris car or any car for that matter, this is the picture of Cowley and its problems which I gained during my visit there.

"Cowley is of course an assembly plant, one factory in the group which comprises the Nuffield organisation. There are four companies in the group which produce cars. There is Cowley, now running on Morris '8s' and '10s'; Wolseley Motors of Birmingham producing a range of '8s', '10s', '12s', '14s' and '18s'; Riley at Coventry with its 1½ litre and 2½ litre saloons; and the M.G. Car Company near

208

Oxford which has two models, the 11 hp sports Midget and 1¼ litre saloon. That makes 11 models for the group as a whole. Stress is laid on long production runs in the motor industry – an aim which Morris Motors has itself. And the policy of the Nuffield organisation is to prune still further the number of types in their future programme.

Group Concentration

"The number of models at present really hides the degree of standardisation – or, perhaps, it would be better to say concentration – which the group has already carried out. The engines branch at Coventry, for instance, makes all engines for the group except those for Riley. The radiators branch at Oxford and Llanelly supplies the whole group and others besides. All axles come from Wolseley. Carburetters for Morris, Wolseley and M.G. come from the S.U. Carburetter Company, a subsidiary. Some motor bodies and a large proportion of the metal pressings are supplied by Nuffield Metal Products of Birmingham and the plant at Llanelly – the balance of the bodies coming from Morris bodies branch at Coventry and from Pressed Steel of Oxford.

"It may seem uneconomic that engines are made in one place, radiators in another, axles somewhere else and so on, and all are brought to Cowley or to one of the other finishing units, to be assembled. But it is one of the accidents of history that William Richard Morris started his cycle shop in Oxford and expanded into the motor industry from there. Today, with all the limitations there are on the movement of labour, there is nothing which can be done about concentrating all the Nuffield works under one roof. In any case, it is doubtful if the economies to be gained makes such a step worthwhile.

Assembly Problems

"Meanwhile, the picture we have is one of a stream of components coming mainly to Cowley where – to take a 10 hp as an example – about 3½ days after a body starts on the production line, it comes off as a finished car. The assembly is done on the moving line principle. The job comes to the man on a conveyor belt which is moving at approximately 2ft 6ins a minute. Each man has a particular task to do. Now, with that type of production the rate at which finished cars come off seems to be dependent on three main factors. First, there must be a regular supply of all components. A minor component might not be so vital, for there is a squad of what might be called 'chasers up' who can put on afterwards any piece within reason – such as the cap of a petrol tank – which happens to be lacking. But in general it is true that a component must be beside the assembly line when it is required.

"Secondly, the output rate depends on the speed at which the line is moving which itself is governed by the length of time it takes a man to do his particular job. Each task on the line takes approximately 5-6 minutes. And thirdly there is the length of the line and the number of men who can work on it. Now there is a limit, of course, to the number of men who can be accommodated, without interfering with each other, around a car at any one moment. That number is roughly four, two on each side. So assuming that the supply of components is adequate, the capacity of the line is governed basically by the speed at which the men work.

Output and Manpower

"Today that speed is *on the average* about 30 per cent less than it was before the war. Think for a moment what that means. If the plant had a capacity before the war of 60 cars and vans an hour, which is approximately what it was, the same plant and the same production methods today would produce only about 40 in the same time. The overheads remain largely the same. Why has productivity fallen? Relations between the management and men appear to be good. There are excellent amenities and social welfare schemes – clubs, medical centres, profit-sharing schemes and the like. The men have the entree to the higher executives with an ease which is not paralleled in many firms. Wages are good; they are rather more than 60 per cent higher on the average than in 1939. There is no trouble with labour unions.

"This fall in the men's effort is indeed a problem and it is difficult to see what the company alone can do to combat it apart, perhaps, from installing more mechanical appliances and modifying the method of production. The men have an incentive to work harder for they are paid on a group piece work system so that any additional effort does mean more money at the end of the week. And they have recently increased their effort on average by 5 per cent.

Appendix

"The 5 per cent increase in labour productivity at Cowley happened in this way. When the production was re-started in 1945 it was found that on average each job took about 35 per cent longer than in 1939. Recently, following the fuel crisis, the staff was asked if it would pull another 5 per cent, which the majority, but not all, agreed to do. Some shops since then have agreed to pull yet another 5 per cent, and if an allowance is made for those who are still working at the 1945 rate, the works as a whole is producing about 5 per cent more effort than it did. Some women in the trimming shops – these are paid on piece rates too – are now doing 80 minutes work in 60 minutes at the 1945 rate of timing. So here and there, there are signs that the position is improving. The men and women are working harder now than they did before the fuel crisis, although there must be in some a belief that extra effort now might mean no job later on. The spirit in the works must, therefore, be good.

Incentive Schemes

"The position is surely this. If there were more goods to buy; if all the men had a home for which furniture could be bought; if, in fact, the possession of money meant more than it does today, then there is little doubt that the desire to earn money would increase. It probably will increase – the Morris executives do not take at all a gloomy view – as time goes on and as new men become more accustomed to working on a moving line, which at the start must be disturbing. But whether the 1939 rate will ever be regained without additional mechanical aids is another matter. The problem of labour productivity is not concentrated at Cowley or anywhere else. It is the country's problem, not a company's, although Morris does appear to be doing all that it can with its incentive and welfare schemes.

"There are about five or six labour unions represented in the works and the company negotiates its agreements with the largest, the A.E.U. Cowley is not a closed shop – few works actually are – and probably no more than 50 per cent of the men or women are members of a labour union. The staff is drawn either from Oxford or the neighbouring towns such as Banbury, Swindon or Reading, and it is difficult to get. The population of the district has an agricultural rather than an industrial background, which produces in some men at any rate a dislike, in daytime, of a roof over their heads. It would be difficult to import labour into the district owing to the lack of housing accommodation. So there appears to be a limit to the expansion which can take place at Cowley, although it is a moot point whether the labour supply is a more difficult problem at the moment than that of components. If there were more labour there could be more cars, if there were more materials. For the management it is one thing after another – wheels were the problem when I was there and the fact that production has gone up and is now at its highest post-war level is a first-class testimonial to the energy which everyone showed.

Cost of British Cars

"Another point of equal importance is that of price. Why do British cars cost so much in relation to pre-war? Their price is about double – why? There seems to be three reasons.

"First, output. If there were more cars coming off the line in a day there would be a greater spread of overheads.

"Secondly, labour. Allowing for the 30 per cent average decline in productivity and the increase in wages, labour costs are up by almost 100 per cent.

"Thirdly, the price of components, which has risen by anything from 70 per cent to well over 300 per cent since 1939. The price of steel bodies, for example, is up by 72 per cent; tyres and tubes by 157 per cent; textiles by 200 per cent; wadding by 330 per cent; electrical equipment by 98 per cent; carpets by 105 per cent – and so it goes on. Nor is that all. For the high price and scarcity of these components is not only pushing up the cost of existing car models, but it is also delaying the introduction of new ones. As the component suppliers have to exert every effort to meet their existing contracts, many of them are reluctant to undertake new ones. And one way of showing that reluctance is to quote a high price. That is an old method of discouraging an order without actually rejecting it. It is still in use. Morris Motors will tell you the story of one of their suppliers who recently quoted a price of 75 per cent higher than the figure they were actually charging for the same article supplied to Morris under another reference.

"New Morris models are coming, although most certainly not this year. (A new M.G. model has just been introduced.) At a guess there will be no major departure from the company's old policy of concentrating its bread and butter lines on the medium size type of car. Morris executives are insistent that they cannot compete with American prices by producing an American type car. It must be complementary to the American types rather than competitive. It must satisfy the home market besides the export demand. And the home market, with the current weight of taxation, its small domestic garages, congested roads and towns, wants a small car. In any case, Morris has about 250,000 firm orders for its current models, 20 per cent from overseas.

Direction of Exports

"The best overseas markets are, and always have been, Australia, New Zealand and India in that order. South Africa is the worst market in the empire and the Americans, who have assembly plants there, are pressing hard to have the tariff raised.

"There has been no reaction so far against the price of the company's major lines although some is expected later on when the Americans have more cars they can offer overseas. At present the Morris '10' is selling at approximately the same price overseas as the Chevrolet or Ford V8, and the ideal proposition in the export company's view would be a car similar to the '10' – perhaps with a little more power – selling at a somewhat lower price than its American rivals. Price, in fact, is going to be a much more important factor in the future, in, say, 18 months' time, when Morris estimate the sellers' market overseas will end. Even today there is a certain resistance to the larger cars which are competing on price with the more luxurious American models.

Price and Volume

"Price and volume, the two are linked together. With a set of dies for a body costing about £250,000 today, any new model must be certain of a large market before it is worthwhile starting. There is more in it even than that. The company must be assured that the flow of supplies will be adequate – that is why Nuffield Mechanisations has postponed production of its tractor. A motor manufacturer must be certain of the government's intentions on, for instance, taxation, which could vitally affect the home market. Private enterprise naturally has to take risks – that is what it is there for.

"It is easy, as we all know, to criticise the motor industry; to say that its prices are too high; that it is taking too much of the country's resources; that it is selling too little overseas and in the wrong markets. The really difficult job is to get the supplies which will ensure an adequate output; to get those supplies at the right price; to increase labour productivity; and to produce a model which will sell at home and overseas against American competition. If a company can do all that, then it is bound to be a leader in the motor industry and remain one."

Index

215

Index